BOXER TO BUSINESSMAN

BOXER TO BUSINESSMAN

How the discipline of being an athlete can help you achieve success as an entrepreneur. Based on a true story.

Angel Carmona

Columbus, Ohio

Boxer To Businessman: How the discipline of being an athlete can help you achieve success as an entrepreneur. Based on a true story.
Published by Gatekeeper Press
2167 Stringtown Rd, Suite 109
Columbus, OH 43123-2989
www.GatekeeperPress.com

Copyright © 2020 by Angel Carmona
All rights reserved. Neither this book, nor any parts within it may be sold or reproduced in any form or by any electronic or mechanical means, including information storage and retrieval systems without permission in writing from the author. The only exception is by a reviewer, who may quote short excerpts in a review.

The cover design, interior formatting, typesetting, and editorial work for this book are entirely the product of the author. Gatekeeper Press did not participate in and is not responsible for any aspect of these elements.

Library of Congress Control Number: 2021940738

ISBN (hardcover): 9781662914409
ISBN (paperback): 9781662914416
eISBN: 9781662914423

Contents

FOREWORD	7
THANK YOU!	9
BOXER TO BUSINESSMAN	11
ROUND 1: GROWING UP	11
ROUND 2: ROCK DID IT	19
ROUND 3: KICKED OUT	27
ROUND 4: CHOICES	35
ROUND 5: THE GROVE	43
ROUND 6: COMEBACK SEASON	57
ROUND 7: TOUCHED	63
ROUND 8: ROCK DID IT, AGAIN!	71
ROUND 9: LIGHTS, CAMERA, ACTION!!!	81
ROUND 10: MURPHY'S LAW	91
ROUND 11: NO PAIN NO GAIN	101
ROUND 12: EXPECT THE UNEXPECTED	111
THE VERDICT: AND THE WINNER IS...	119
FINAL THOUGHT	125

FOREWORD

I wrote this book for you, the athletes around the world, the rising superstars and soon to be champions that will one day undergo some unforeseen circumstances; circumstances that will threaten your livelihood as professional athletes, and in some cases even end your potentially thriving careers in the sports world. Whether you find yourself thrown off-course by an injury, lack of discipline, the wrong associations or choices, I'm here to tell you that there's still success on the other side of tragedy! I'm living proof that there is. The principles of success that made you a good athlete are the same in every area of life. As long as you consistently apply what you've learned, success will be inevitable.

I'll tell you one thing, it wasn't easy being this vulnerable. Pulling back the curtain and telling stories that only my immediate family knows about, was as scary and intimidating as you could imagine. I didn't ask any of my siblings for permission to tell my side of these stories. As I wholeheartedly believe, two people can experience the exact same situation, yet have two completely different perspectives in the end. Though I may have left out a few stories in order not to incriminate myself, nor anyone else mentioned, nothing in this book is fabricated. As a matter of fact, when I asked one of my brothers if i should dumb it down and make it *PG-13*, he told me that my life was *Rated R* and why would

I dare sugarcoat what I've been through. I know I will lose some followers after I expose my past with full transparency, but sobeit.

I didn't write this book to glorify my past and all the "bad things" I did. I want you to learn from my mistakes and understand where I came from, in comparison to where I'm at in life. My suggestion is that you take notes as you read along because there are lots of life lessons, and or business principles in every chapter of this book. I hope you don't get motivated and inspired, because motivation and inspiration will only get you started. It is discipline and determination that'll keep you going. And if you're the only person that changes their life through reading this book, it'll be worth all the judgement and ridicule I'm about to receive from everyone else.

THANK YOU!

I want to dedicate this book to someone who doesn't get the credit they deserve, my boxing coach, five times world champion, Robert Daniels. Thank you for being a father figure growing up, and a true role model. You taught me so much about discipline and invited me to church. I want to celebrate you and give you your flowers while you're still here.

Thank you, Charles James (Carlos), for holding me accountable to writing this book. Everyone told me I should write one, but you actually held me accountable. Thank you for pushing me. Thank you for investing your time and wisdom into me. Thank you for painting this vision and most importantly helping me turn it into reality. I'm grateful to have someone like you in my corner. Thank you for reminding me, I can be THAT GUY! I appreciate you!

Thank you to Rocky! Thank you for changing my life, twice! I'm forever indebted to you brother!

Thanks to my brothers from another mother, Keith, for teaching me how to write, and Kel, for taking me in when I had nowhere to go. Love.

Special thank you to all the doubters, haters, and non-believers. You were the fuel to my fire!

Last but not least, thank you to all my mentors! Way too many to name, but you know who you are. Your knowledge and wisdom over the last decade has shaped me to be the man I am today and the man I'll become tomorrow.

BOXER TO BUSINESSMAN

GROWING UP

As Children We Are Products of Our Environments, as Adults We Are Products of Our Decisions

All I remember hearing was the sound of glass breaking, and a woman screaming at the top of her lungs. I ran out of my room to meet my siblings, my older brother and my younger brother and sister, standing still at the top of the stairs. There, I stood in shock, staring at my mom bleeding from her mouth as she laid on the floor. My dad stood over her, drunk, with blood on his white Versace dress shirt. I had started to get used to it; this had been happening every other night, if not every night, for the past few months. Just about a week prior, my older brother and I were in the kitchen while my dad beat the brakes off my mom. It was so bad that we each grabbed a butcher knife to try to help our mom out. We ended up chickening out, in fear of what our dad might do to us.

I was about nine years old. We were living in Santo Domingo, in the Dominican Republic. I was the second oldest, each of us roughly two years apart. My parents looked up at us, and my dad uttered the words, "We're getting a divorce." Just like that, 13 years of marriage gone down the drain. I was instantly heartbroken, just like any kid who wants their parents to have a lifelong thriving marriage. The next words that came out of his mouth were "Choose who you want to live with, your mom or your dad?" It seemed as if the answers from my siblings came in slow motion. They all chose my mom. But somehow, I chose my dad. Growing up, I was always the closest to him and so inspired by his work ethic. But he paused for a while, and then said that he didn't want to separate me from my siblings, and that I should go with my mom.

At the time, I just couldn't comprehend what my mom was doing wrong, for my dad to knock the teeth out of her mouth and slam her head through a glass table. He was a heavyweight and had some prior boxing experience. It didn't add up why he would beat my petite mom, as if she were a grown man. It just didn't make sense, she was so slender and weighed about 120lbs soaking wet. Today, I come to understand, she wasn't doing anything wrong. It was my dad who had the flaws all along.

My dad was the hardest working man I had ever known. He started shining shoes at the age of 6. He is most definitely the reason for my ambition and hustler's spirit. He met my mom when she was fourteen years old; he didn't have much, but he asked her to marry him anyway. My mom was the only child, and her mother, my grandma, was married to a very wealthy American businessman. When my mom married my dad, her stepfather (the wealthy businessman), moved my parents to Florida where they would start to build their life.

My dad would work miscellaneous jobs here and there just to provide for his family, which was growing. My life before the age of nine is very vague, practically a blur. I just know that I was born in Miami, FL, in 1987 and that over the next nine years we moved a lot: from Miami, to New York, back to Santo Domingo. My dad lived under his means and saved up almost all his income from working 2 and 3 jobs at a time, with hopes to one day return to the Dominican Republic and invest all his hard-earned money into real estate. And that's exactly what he did. By the time he was in his mid-20's, my dad was a self-made multi-millionaire. He owned over two dozen apartment units, a dozen cars, and two convenient stores. We lived in a 4 bed 2 ½ bathroom mansion, with a basketball court and a guest house in the backyard. He built an in-home bar that carried some of the finest rum and whiskeys the country had to offer. We had a maid that would clean and iron. We even had a nanny who lived with us, to help my mom with cooking and raising us.

We would frequently take vacations to lavish resorts. He paid the government to lay tar on the dirt road on the entire street where we lived. And he paid them to put light poles around the entire neighborhood. When it was time to go to the beach on the weekends, he would invite all of the neighbors, and cover all the transportation costs, as well as all the food. If "Go Big Or Go Home" was a person, it would've definitely been my dad. During Christmas time, he'd buy toys, not just for his own kids, but for all the kids in the entire neighborhood. This lasted for about 3 years. So, you can see why he was my hero and why I admired him so much.

But with all that money, came the haters. So, in order to protect his family, he had guns galore, and he wasn't afraid to remind people of his power from time to time. Occasionally, he'd light the night skies on fire just to remind people who was the man in charge. Overall, most people had love for him. Or at least pretended to.

One summer, he sent my mom, my older brother, and my little sister on a vacation to New York city for a few weeks. During that time, him, his best friend, my younger brother and I took a road trip around the island of the Dominican Republic. By now you can tell my dad was a pretty popular guy around town. On a random day on our road trip, we stopped by an ice cream shop and he sent me to go pay. While inside, I overheard a man talking aloud to himself, saying how much he hated my dad and that he was going to kill him next time he saw him. The guy was clearly unaware I was his son and heard every word he said behind his back. When I got back in the car, I told my dad exactly what I heard, as he slowly drove away. He immediately made a U-turn and pulled back in front of the ice cream shop. There, the guy stood outside the store, talking loudly, and we sat in the car behind tinted windows. My dad pulled out his gun, cocked it back and handed it to me. He said step out, point at him, but don't get too close, and say "Who are you going to kill now, motherfucker?", in Spanish. I stepped out of the car and did exactly as I was told. The guy laughed and said, "No kid, I was just playing." My dad rolled down his window, instructed me to get back in, and told the guy, "Next time I hear you talking shit, it's going to be me hopping out the car and I'm not just going to aim." I was but seven or eight years old.

On that same trip, I walked in on him sleeping with other women. But I kept my mouth shut, just because I didn't want my parents to split. Even though, as we all know, what's done in the dark, will soon come to light. And as the years went by, the money and power seemed to get to my dad's head more and more.

He loved watching Tyson fights. And alpha male movies like Indiana Jones. He was obsessed with documentaries on Rafael Trujillo, a tyrant who ruled the Dominican Republic for over 30 years, killing anyone who stood in his way. They called him the Dominican version of Hitler. During his time, in the '50s, he amassed a net worth of over $800M, an equivalent of over $5B in today's money. My dad would watch documentaries on him almost every damn week, as if he were studying his ways. Maybe that's the reason he felt in some ways, UNTOUCHABLE.

Later in life, one of my mentors taught me that pride comes before the fall. And indeed, my dad was prideful. This tends to happen to many people who go from the bottom to the top. My dad had gone from barely having clothes on his back and shoes on his feet, to wearing Versace — almost exclusively. And on New Year's Eve, he would dress me and all my siblings in Oscar De La Renta, the world-renowned Dominican fashion designer. He went from living in the slums in a house made from tin, to owning land and real estate. In the '90s, our home alone had over $100k worth of marble floors! All of the furniture in the house, including the stairs, was made from mahogany wood. A wood that's not only expensive but also rare, so much so that in 2003 it was actually made illegal to own or trade. My dad had also built a well in the backyard, and we had generators, too. This was all in a city where water and electricity cuts happen multiple times a week, for days at a time. We had an air conditioning unit in every room. Even a satellite on the roof that gave us access to U.S. channels. To top it all off, all four of us were enrolled in private school, my dad paying the tuition fees in full at the beginning of every year. Now, you may ask yourself,

"What's the big deal?" Just understand that these types of amenities were not common in a third world country in the mid 90's!

Yet as the years passed, my dad got more and more abusive. Not just with my mom, but with me and my siblings as well. My older brother would always get it the worse. He would even punch him if he didn't eat his food. And on certain occasions, he hit him with a metal bat just for not eating his vegetables. He used that same bat to hit my grandma once after they got into a heated argument about him physically abusing my mom.

I recall one weekend, me and my brothers asked my dad to play outside, and he said it was ok but not to make any noise because he was trying to take a nap. We went downstairs, and within a few minutes, I did a cartwheel, and I accidentally kicked my brother in the eye with my heel. He instantly started to scream, hysterically. I tried my best to calm him down, as any sibling would do after injuring their brother or sister, but it was too late. My dad ran downstairs with a thick leather lifting belt he would wear to work in construction projects. He looked at my little brother and asked him what happened. My brother then pointed at me and said I kicked him. My dad made us line up and lean over on the 10 ft tall metal garage gate, and he started to take out all his anger and frustration on us. After almost 10 minutes of screaming, the neighbors became alarmed and started to approach our house begging my dad to stop, through the gate. He did. When I finally went upstairs, took my shirt off, and checked my back in the mirror, about 70% of the skin on my back was peeled off. To this day, I wonder how it can be that I don't have any scars on my back from that afternoon.

When my mom saw me, I could tell she was fed up. She wanted to leave, and she had been planning to leave, but stayed out of fear of what my dad might do if she even tried. Towards the end, he started an affair with a neighbor's wife. They were a family from New York that had recently moved near us. Once my mom found out about the affair, that was the last straw for her. She did everything in her power for my dad to give her a divorce.

After my dad decided to let my mom keep all the kids that night, my parents agreed to sell the house and all the cars and split the revenue. Within a month, my dad liquidated everything for pennies on the dollar, and still managed to amass over $1,000,000 in cash. He then gave my mom $2000 to move back to Miami with us and start her life over. But not before one last beating.

Even though I grew up in a toxic environment, I vowed not to let my abusive upbringing shape my views on marriage and parenting. When I got older, I decided that I would never lay a hand on a woman, no matter the circumstances. Nor would I ever beat my kids in order to discipline them. Over 20 years later, I'm blessed to say I have never physically assaulted any woman. I just refuse to inflict the level of pain my dad made my mom endure.

ROCK DID IT

My Introduction to Boxing

When we landed in Miami in '97, we went to live with some of my dad's siblings. We lived with them for a couple of months before my mom found a small 2 bed 1 bath house in North Miami for the five of us. It was almost immediately that I saw a change in my moms' demeanor. My mom had never worked before. Her only job while married to my dad had been to raise us. But it suddenly felt as if she went from caring for us, to us being "baggage." Shortly after we moved into our new home, my mom reconnected with her childhood best friend. Before I knew it, she was visiting the house and asking my mom to go to a New Year's Eve party with her. I recall thinking to myself, "My mom would never leave us during this special holiday. We always welcome the new year together, as a family." Plus, we were only kids; my older brother was just eleven years old. But I was wrong, and I was also heartbroken. My mom left that night and didn't return until around 3 or 4 a.m..

Soon, my mom started working at a retail store in a mall for $5.15/hr. Not long after, she met a man who also worked there and they started dating. My mom started bringing him over to the house frequently. Though he was a cool guy, I wasn't mentally and emotionally ready to replace my dad with another man. Despite everything he'd done to my mom and to us, deep inside, I would constantly pray for a miracle, that my mom would forgive my dad, that they'd get back together, and that we'd live happily ever after as a family. That prayer was never answered, as my mom ended up getting engaged to her new boyfriend. I once again was in disbelief.

My mom's new boyfriend would periodically invite us over to his grandmother's house for different occasions and parties. He had a pretty big family, and that's where we ended up meeting all his cousins. One Sunday morning, all his younger cousins were playing in the front yard. One of them was a 13-year-old guy, who went by the name of Rocky. This guy stood out from the rest of the cousins. He dressed sharp, his haircut was sharp, and he was physically more fit than the rest of us. As we stood around, he took off his shirt and said, "I go to this boxing gym, and I bet none of you can do the kind of exercises I do there!" Then he dropped to the floor and started demonstrating the different types of exercises, from diamond push ups, to six inches, to mountain climbers and crunches, and many more. I was so intrigued. The competitiveness in me couldn't stay quiet, I blurted out, "I bet I could!" He looked at me and laughed. Then he continued to explain how difficult the routines were, over the next hour or so.

I was small. At ten years old, I only weighed 80 lbs. The whole car ride home, I kept trying to convince my mom and her boyfriend to let me go to this boxing gym Rocky goes to. My older brother also felt challenged, so since he was interested, and much heavier and older, my mom gave him permission to go. I thought it was unfair, so I was upset. But after my brother came home from his first day at the gym, exhausted, he explained that the minimum age requirement to join the gym was eleven years old. I was pissed. So I asked my brother if he could show me a couple of the exercises he did at the gym, so I could attempt to do them at home. Just like I thought, I knew I could handle the pain! I patiently waited all summer to turn old enough to be allowed in the gym. Meanwhile, I kept training at home, or at least I thought that was what I was doing.

One day my brother came home from the gym really excited. He told me that Rocky and he had convinced the boxing coach to allow me to attend the gym. He told him that I was just a few months shy of turning eleven years old, and that I had been working out all summer in preparation for the gym. All we then had to do was convince my mom and her boyfriend to let me go. And once she saw our excitement, she finally granted me permission to start boxing.

I had been waiting for that moment for months. I remember walking into the boxing gym like a kid in a candy store. I ran over to the punching bags and turned around at Rocky and my brother asking, "What are we doing today guys? Hitting the heavy bag?" I then ran over to the ring asking, "Or are we putting on the gloves and throwing hands?" Then, I went over to the speed bag and yelled "No — I want to hit the speed bag first!" The coach looked at Rocky and my brother and they all started laughing simultaneously. I was so confused; I didn't understand what was so funny. The coach then grabbed me by my shoulder and walked me over to some mirrors mounted on the wall. He then started to explain the importance of having a proper stance, and the most important punch, the jab.

For the next 3 months, I would come in the gym and spend the first two hours in front of the mirror practicing my V Form aka my boxing stance, followed by another two hours in the "hot room", where we would perform those excruciating exercises that Rocky deemed impossible months earlier. Lastly, we'd end the day with a 2-mile run around the block. For the first few months, not one bag was hit, not one round was spent sparring in the ring. That's when I learned that endurance and foundation were the two most important factors that will make or break a boxer. Like anything in life, whether that's boxing, business, or anything new, you're going to be bad before you're good, good before you're great, and great before you're the best!

Not long after I started, my brother stopped coming to the gym with me. Rocky moved to New Jersey to pursue his career with another trainer. And my mom and her fiancé broke off their engagement (she blamed domestic violence). I, on the other hand, stayed very consistent and started to take boxing very seriously. I started competing in amateur bouts. I won some, I lost some. After a couple of years of going to the gym 5 and 6 days a week, I kept working on my skills in preparation for my next match, a state championship!

One night after a hard day at the gym, I was in my room getting ready to lie down and rest so that I could do it all over again the next day. That's when I heard my mom call my name, saying I had a phone call. I figured it was my coach, calling to say that I left something in his truck. But when I walked in her room, to my surprise, she said it was my dad…

I was so shocked and so happy! I had a million thoughts running through my head within seconds of grabbing the phone. This would be the first time we would speak since the divorce. My initial thought was "Oh man, maybe they're going to reconcile and get back together!" Then I instantly shifted my thinking and told myself "No! I have to tell him I started boxing, he's going to be so happy," considering he also used to box at one point in time. I grabbed the phone, and after I said hello, the first thing my dad said after "How are you?" was, "Your mom told me you started boxing. I think you should quit. You're too small, leave that for your older brother, he's much heavier than you." I was so disappointed. I just couldn't believe he didn't have faith in me. I said "OK" and handed the phone back to my mom. I was infuriated.

My dad didn't know it but all he had done was add fuel to the fire already burning inside of me. His lack of faith in me drove me to work out ten times harder, be ten times more focused, and become ten times more skilful as a fighter. As a result, over the next 7 years I won 10 different state championships at my weight class. And I never wanted to talk to him again.

By then, I had started to gain notoriety in school. Growing up in Florida, most guys my age choose to play football because of the good weather. I chose to go against the grain and box instead, making me one of the few, if not the only one in my class to do so. Up to that point, my mom had made us move practically every year since the divorce. Hence, I had to switch schools every year and start from scratch when it came to making friends and getting into relationships (staying in touch was harder back then since cell phones weren't very popular). Thankfully, because of my boxing skills, I had no problem getting popular in every school I went to. All I had to do was tell someone I boxed, they would tell everyone, and then some dummy would try to challenge me in something we called Slap Boxing (which was basically boxing with open hands), and I simply had to make an example out of them by "whooping their ass" as we said back then.

One day, when I walked in the gym, my coach pulled me to the side and told me that I was doing great, to keep up the great work and stay consistent. He also said that at the rate I was going, I could perhaps have a chance at entering the Olympic trials. I was so excited! I couldn't believe this went from wanting to prove to Rocky that I could do some exercises, to wanting to prove my dad wrong, to being in the talks to represent my weight class at US Olympic trials! Once that happened, I was sure that I would be a world champion by age 21!

KICKED OUT

Sometimes Our Biggest Setbacks Our God's Set Up for Our Comebacks

By 2003, we had moved into public housing aka "the projects." We lived in a 4 bed 2 bath two story apartment unit, and the rent was only $24.00 a month. We had no vehicle during that time and we were on welfare. On the first of the month we would receive a couple hundred dollars worth of food stamps. My mom had convinced us that moving there, for one year max, would help her save enough money for a down payment to buy us a house. But four years had already gone by.

After years of being on a waiting list, my mom had finally got the phone call she had been waiting for for so long, her caseworker telling her that she had been accepted into the affordable housing program. When the first availability showed up , we had two choices; accept it and relocate, or go to the back of the waiting list. So when the first apartment became available, my mom jumped on it right away.

This particular development happened to be in Liberty city, Miami, in the heart of an area called Brownsville, and the projects there were called "Brown Sub." This was, at the time, one of the worst places you could live anywhere in Miami. If I could describe in one word the feeling I felt on moving day, that word would be DISAPPOINTED. I just couldn't believe that my mom would settle for living in such heinous conditions, coming from where we came from. I had a strong feeling of disgust in my stomach. My initial thought was, "Why the hell didn't my dad let me stay with him?" We went from living lavish, to living on government assistance.

The Brown Sub projects were infested with crime. There were drug dealers literally on our back door steps, selling drugs 24/7. It didn't take a genius to realize that our apartment was right smack in the middle of a dope hole. No wonder our apartment had become vacant. Everyone from crackheads to prostitutes would come around the clock fiending for their next fix. Gunshots would ring out every other night, just as commonly as birds would chirp in the morning.

I recall one weekday evening, at around 10:00 p.m., there was a shootout, and the bullet from an AK-47 came through the window and blew off part of the headboard from my mom's bed. Luckily, she had gotten up two minutes earlier to wash a couple of dishes that were left in the kitchen sink. Coming home from school, I had to walk past junkies who were strung out on the corner. There was only one good thing about living in Brown Sub: I was only 2.5 miles away from the boxing gym!

    I decided to spend as much time as possible at the gym, after school. I was so focused and determined to work hard and be able to move my mom and siblings out of the hood. My boxing coach at the time was a guy by the name of Robert Daniels. He was a former 5X cruiserweight world champion, and the first boxing world champion to come out of the state of Florida. At the time, my coach was the most successful person I knew. He seemed to have his life together. He was accomplished, financially stable, married with two kids, and a devoted church goer. Within a few months of meeting him, he invited me to his church. Perhaps because I admired him so much, I ended up committing to that church and eventually I even got baptized. Due to his Christian beliefs, my coach's boxing alias was "the preacher man". He was a really humble guy.

    After my daily workouts, I became accustomed to assisting my coach in helping to train other up and coming boxers. School would end at 2:20 p.m. , and I would be at the gym at 3:00 p.m. sharp to help open. I would work out for two hours, and then around 5:00 p.m., when most people would arrive, I would shift from training myself, to being a trainer. My skills had gotten so advanced, that he would let me train anyone from a little kid to a grown adult. In all honesty, what I was trying to do was to stay as far away as possible from my home environment.

I remember one day I decided to walk to the gym because my bike had a flat tire. Because I contributed so much to the gym through my volunteer work, my coach would always do his best to help me as much as he could. On that particular day, he offered to drop me off home since he knew I walked and was exhausted from training myself and training others. I was so embarrassed of where I lived, that I didn't want to tell him. But he insisted on dropping me off, so I obliged. It was a short ride home but seemed like forever. As we pulled up, we seemed to be driving in slow motion. As we came to a stop, I turned to look at the facial expression on my coach's face, I could see the fear in his eyes. He looked at me and said "Boy, you better be careful out here in these streets!" Then, he busted out laughing. My coach had also grown up in the hood, so he wasn't scared for himself. But he *was* fearful for me. And as much as he tried to make light of it at that moment, he was fearful of what would happen to me if the streets got a hold of me.

A couple of days went by, and I had gotten my bike fixed. Right before I left the gym, my coach pulled me aside and told me something I would never forget and live by for the rest of my life. He said "Angel, the two hours you workout here in the gym don't make you a champion, it's what you do the rest of the 22 hours when you are not training that's gonna determine your success. Are you out there staying out late, trying to make a quick buck, sleeping around with multiple women, smoking and drinking? Your lifestyle outside of the gym will show up when you step in that ring. Be careful son, there's nothing good in those streets!" I took heed and listened... Or at least I thought I did.

After someone stole my bike from the backyard, I would every now and then find reasons not to walk all the way to the gym. On those days, I would hang outside and get to know some of my neighbors. One of them was a kid named Kel. He would always walk around with a basketball, dribbling everywhere he went. He had dreams of making it to the NBA, which was interesting to me since, with his dreads, he stood about 5'8. But he had the confidence of someone 6'6. With him dreaming of a basketball career and me dreaming of being a World Boxing champion, we got along really well. From time to time, he would pick out another kid in the neighborhood and ask them to challenge me in a slap boxing match. All the dope boys would gather around and bet money on who they thought would win. I would never let them down.

The day finally came when my mom decided to move out of the Brown Sub projects. Her and her new boyfriend, a Marine veteran, found a house to rent about 2 miles West of where we lived. The day after the move, my mom demanded that I skip the gym and come straight home to help unpack all the boxes and help set up the new house. So, when the next day came, I was walking home from school and I realized that the new house was twice as far as the old one. Like any given day, the weather in Miami is between 90-100 degrees. That day was no different, so I decided to stop by Kel's house to cool off and wait for the sun to go down so that I could continue going home. I ended up falling asleep on the couch and waking up at around 9:30 p.m.. I was about a 20-minute walk from my mom's new spot, so I asked Kel to walk with me halfway so we could mastermind about getting rich.

By that time, the random days of skipping the gym had become more frequent. I would hang out with Kel, and he would introduce me to different kinds of rap music, which always worked to motivate us to get rich sooner rather than later. Us being rich and famous became the common topic of most of our conversations. That night was no different. We wanted to be rich so bad, we even dabbled in the thought of dropping out of high school. He was a sophomore, I was halfway through my senior year.

When I got home that night, I walked straight into my room. My mom followed behind me almost immediately. She started screaming at me saying how I was so selfish and irresponsible for not coming to help out with the move. She then slapped me so hard and told me to go back to where I came from, grab all my stuff and to never ever come back! It took every ounce of discipline in me not to let my boxing reflex takeover and hit her back. My eyes instantly got watery.

I felt so disrespected. I started to pack all my clothes, so that I could leave her house then and there. I didn't know where I was going to go. How could she do this to me? She knew I was bound for the Olympic trials. I was afraid. I was only 16.

After I packed all my J's and fitted caps, and all my other belongings, I walked out the house and immediately called Kel. I told him what had happened and without hesitation he said that I could move in with him. He told me he'd meet me halfway to help me with my bags and then we would walk to his house together and explain the situation to his mom, Ms. Patricia.

CHOICES

The Choices We Make Will Eventually Make Us!

Kel was basically born and raised in Brown Sub. A world that was foreign to me was actually normal to him. He practically knew all the drug dealers by name, what territory belonged to who, and who was a real shooter or a pretender. Unbeknownst to me, Kel lived with his mom, Ms. Patricia, alongside his 3 brothers and 3 sisters, in an apartment the same size as the one my mom had just moved us out of — 4 bed 2 bath. Oh, and one of his sisters had her four kids living there as well.

His oldest brother was fresh out of prison, after having served a few years for drug trafficking charges. The second oldest, Keith, had also just gotten out of prison a year earlier. He was arrested for shooting a gun in a school zone during school hours, but was ultimately charged with an armed robbery that he didn't commit. He was sentenced to 6 years at the age of 14. He was now 21. Keith was 6 ft tall, about 200 lbs, had a mouth full of gold teeth, and was in the beginning stages of growing dreadlocks. Kel introduced me to Keith when he first got out and told me that was his "mil ticket outta the hood." Keith started rapping when he first went to prison, and had an undeniable talent. I had no doubt, one day, he would make it big. And the last brother, around my age, had just gotten out of a detention facility, for an incident at his high school.

When we walked through the door the day that I went to move in with them, Kel's mom was in the kitchen making dinner. I didn't know what to expect and was nervous to see how she'd react to her youngest son bringing a friend to live with them. But as soon as Ms. Patricia turned around, she gave me a big smile and a hug, and asked me if I was hungry. She fed me as if I was one of her own kids.

Ms. Patricia was the sweetest lady I had ever met. She was a single parent, doing her best to provide for her kids. She worked full time as a bus aide for special needs children. She would wake up everyday at 4 am to go to work and would never miss a day. That night she consoled me and assured me everything would be alright. She told me I could sleep in the living room on one couch, and Kel could sleep on the other.

The next morning, me and Kel got up early to go to school. I had so much on my mind, I was really stressed out about what I was going to do moving forward. As I walked with Kel to his bus stop, we were listening to a song on his CD player. Long story short, the lyrics to the song went as follows, "Why go to school, to graduate in debt, so that you then have to get a job making $30k a year, to then have to pay back your student loans? How were you supposed to travel the world and buy exotic cars on that salary?" Me and Kel looked at each other, and decided to drop out on the spot.

Not only did I have a lot on my mind, but in all honesty, I was embarrassed to go back to school with no lunch money, unable to get any new clothes, etc.. I had established a nice reputation throughout my years in high school. I was voted one of the best dressed and most popular kids in school. So I didn't want anyone to be saying I "fell off." Maybe it was pride and ego, maybe not. Call it what you want, but when you grow up in the inner city of Miami, people take the dressing game seriously. And if you came half stepping, you'd get roasted, or "ranked on" as we say in Miami, to the point of no return. And I wasn't trying to get into a fight because of peer pressure.

As we walked back to the house, I asked Kel what we were going to do to make money. He said he didn't know but he had an idea. When we walked in the house, he told me to follow him into his big brother's room, where he then lifted the mattress, and he grabbed two hand guns, a 9MM and a Glock 40 Cal. He told me to hold one of them, and I immediately declined. The last time I held a gun was when I was with my dad, after that I had been so into boxing that I saw no reason to ever need a gun. So after he saw I wasn't interested in holding the gun he blurted out laughing "What? Are you scared?" I said "Of course I'm not scared", so I grabbed it. Then he said "Ok, if all else fails, we could always use these if it came down to making money." I said "Cool" and handed him back the gun.

That same night, Kel and I were walking to the corner store to grab a snack. We saw police car lights and heard sirens, but we ignored them since it was pretty common, especially since the store was also a dope hole. When we walked in, I stayed by the register and Kel went to the back of the store to get his items. After we paid and started walking back, halfway to the house Kel pulled out a plastic container of what appeared to be an empty jar of seasoning salt, and excitedly said, "Fool, I found a bomb in the back of the store!"

By "fool", he meant "bro", and by "bomb" he meant a container where drug dealers keep their drugs, so that they're not on them the entire time — just in case a cop randomly tries to search them and so that the drugs can't be pinned on them, legally. They will usually keep the bomb close by, and when a junkie comes for their fix, they'll simply go and get what they need and keep the rest in the stash. They would also toss or hide the bomb if they were being chased by a cop, and then come back for it later or when they got out of jail for fleeing.

Clueless of what he was talking about, I asked what it was, and he briefly explained it. Then he suggested we get rid of everything, before we got back home, just in case his mom didn't allow us back outside. When he opened it, the bomb had about $300 worth of crack, aka "hard", and coke, aka "soft". So we came up with a strategy, known today as "short stopping". Simply put, we stood in the route "custies" (short for "customers") would take on their way to their regular drug dealer, and we served them up first, before they got to their usual guy. Short stopping is very dangerous and can get you shot and even killed for trespassing onto other dealers' territory. Kel knew this, but he didn't care, so neither did I. He stood at one end of an apartment building, I stood at the other end, and we stopped every customer we saw. Some said no, some said yes. The ones that said yes were mostly buying bundles, leading us to sell out within 45 minutes. I guess it's safe to say "the trap was jumping" and our plan was working! Kel gave me 40% and we called it a night. We felt like we were winning for our first day of dropping out, and that God had blessed our decision by putting that bomb in our path.

About two weeks passed and nothing major had happened for us since then. Kel and I were still without work and Ms. Patricia was putting the pressure on us to get a job or go back to school. One night, as we were walking home from pretending to be out all day looking for a job, we noticed a big crowd gathering in the parking lot. As we got closer, we noticed it was one of Kel's sisters preparing to fight another girl from the neighborhood. Within seconds of us arriving, his sister popped off. The crowd was screaming and cheering for who they thought would win, as was usual with fights in the hood. After about a minute of the girls locking arms, Kel's middle sister decided to jump in the fight. The crowd went into immediate uproar. Right as the fight was about to turn into a full out brawl, Kel's brother, Keith, pulled out a gun and shot twice in the air. The fight broke up, and the crowd scattered instantly.

    We ran home, just like everyone else did, when we heard the cop sirens. Keith ran upstairs to put the gun away. The rest of us stayed in the living room explaining to Ms. Patricia and Kel's oldest sister what had just happened. Before we knew it, 30 minutes had passed by and we were all just laughing about how everything went down. There were about 10 of us in the living room, including Kel's 7 year old niece, his 2 year old twin nieces, and his 3 month old nephew. Then out of nowhere, we heard what we thought were fireworks. We then realized that they were gunshots. First they hit the metal door. Then they came through the living room windows. We all sprinted upstairs while doing our best to shield the babies. After about 15 seconds, the shooting stopped. We noticed blood on the floor. I got grazed in my arm and Kel got grazed in the knee. Thankfully, the kids and the rest of the family were fine and untouched. Keith jumped over everyone in the stairway with two guns, one in each hand, and opened the front door to shoot back at whoever had done this to his home and family. But it was too late, the perpetrators had already sped off. Miss Patricia called the cops. When the detectives showed up, they found 45 bullet shells in the front yard. Keith was livid and so were the rest of the boys.

That night, we didn't sleep. We stayed up all night, each taking turns with the guns ready to protect the family by any means necessary. I remember it like it was yesterday, Keith and the oldest brother came to me around 4:00 a.m. and told me it was my turn to guard the house. He told me the mindset I needed to have was, "It's either them or us." Then, they handed me a gun and Kel another. Lucky for them, the shooters never returned that night.

For the next two days, we repeated the same strategy until we were able to pack up and move to another apartment. The fastest option was to move into Kel's oldest sister's duplex. She had been living with her mom because her light bill was past due and they had shut off her electricity, which made it difficult to live there — especially with young children. It was a 2 bed 1 bath for the 13 of us, but we had no other option; we had to make this work.

When we arrived at the location, I couldn't believe where she was renting. There were only one or two places in Liberty City where the crime rate was worse than Brown Sub, and Little Haiti was one of them.

At one point, Little Haiti was considered the murder capital of America. The neighborhood also made frequent appearances on the hit TV show The First 48. More drugs were moved through and from there than any other area in Liberty City, and probably all of Miami.

Ms. Patricia and Kel's sisters moved out again after a month of saving money, but she told all the boys we had to figure out on our own what we were going to do and where we were going to go. Kel's two older brothers had jobs at a hotel in South Beach. Kel and I would sit home all day and think of what to do, while we waited all day for his oldest brother to come home and give us $4 a day so that we could eat our only meal of the day: a sausage sandwich for $1.50 and a $0.50 jungle juice. This lasted for weeks.

One day Kel and I got fed up, and sick of waiting to eat. So we grabbed the guns and decided we were going to rob the next person we saw walking outside. We dressed up in all black, went outside, and after a few minutes, we noticed a guy walking down the block. We started walking towards him, and as we crept closer, we noticed he was a student. We didn't care. But right as we were about to pull out the guns, he walked into the school grounds and got away. No one else passed by for hours. So we just went home and continued waiting for Kel's brother.

We lived in that duplex with no electricity for a little over two months. Until one day, Kel begged his mom to let me and him come live with them in their new apartment in Coconut Grove, FL. She agreed, as long as we got jobs. We moved out that same day.

THE GROVE

What the Lick Read?

Kel and I had become family. Even though I was 6'1, light skinned, with waves, and he was a bit darker and shorter with dreads, no one would dare question if we were real brothers; we were that tight. Within a couple of days of moving to Coconut Grove, me and Kel were walking home from the corner store and he noticed a sign on the window of a local restaurant that said, "Now Hiring." Kel told me I should go inside and ask about the job. I thought about the promise I made to his mom, and I walked in reluctantly. The manager told me to come back in the morning to speak with the owner for an interview. The next morning, I showed up at 9 a.m. sharp and met the owner of House Of Wings. We didn't know it at the time, but it was the most popular restaurant in town, with plenty of awards to show for it.

Mr. Muhammad was an ex-con from D.C. who had relocated to South Florida and converted to Islam. He had started a few businesses, but the two that thrived the most were House Of Wings and Headliners Barbershop, which were next door to each other. He had a thing for the finer things in life and his designer wardrobe proved it. During the interview, he asked me what my story was. I briefly explained how I was boxing but then my mom kicked me out, forcing me to drop out of school and get a job. He then told me the next four questions would determine whether I'd be hired or not. He then went on to ask me what "desire", "dedication", "determination" and "discipline" meant to me. I answered his questions to the best of my ability and all he said was "You're hired, see you in the morning!"

The place was booming from open to close. Phones ringing off the hook. The line outside the door was a sign of how busy the kitchen constantly was. I did everything from prepping, to cooking, to cleaning, and would eventually end up on the register. After a couple of weeks, I noticed the hiring sign was still up, so I referred Kel to the owner. He was also interviewed and hired on the spot. House Of Wings was the go-to after school spot for most students. Due to the popularity of the wings, celebrities like NBA players James Posey and Dorell Wright (among many others) would frequent the place. Mr. Muhammad was well-known, and

I even witnessed Birdman and Slim, the founders of Cash Money Records walk in there once. This type of notoriety made H.O.W. *the* place to work for the average teenager in The Grove. The fact that Kel and I got jobs there before everyone else made all the girls in the neighborhood want us, and all the guys envious of us. We had no idea of the problems that would arise from this underlying jealousy.

There's something about being from Miami. No matter where you are in the country, if you say you're from Miami, you get instant respect from the guys, and instant admiration from the girls. That said, in Miami, or anywhere in South Florida, when you say you're from The City (Liberty City), you still get admiration from the girls, but you get envy and hate from the guys. During these times, Kel and I would roam the streets regularly shirtless or with a tank top and our pants sagging. When we did wear shirts, it was always 3-4X bigger than our original sizes, which back then, those types of long tees were in style. We thought we were cool, and though the elderly would tell us to put on a shirt and pick our pants up, we never listened for whatever reason. It was normal to us and our friends, plus we wanted our gun handle to poke out so people knew not to play with us. We always wondered why we were stereotyped, but all we had to do was look in the mirror.

Though we were only making minimum wage, Kel and I started to work a lot of overtime, which allowed us to stack our money and make moves pretty fast. We were able to get our wardrobe together, much of which we had left behind when we quickly moved out after the house was shot up. We put our money together and bought a '97 Chevy Caprice. And most importantly, we were helping Ms. Patricia out with the bills. But the word was getting out quick, how two guys from The City were taking over The Grove. So the more haters we gained, the more guns we bought, and it all made the girls from The Grove go crazy for us.

One day, Kel and I were walking from the store, when a random guy hopped the fence of his backyard and stood in our way with a gun in his hand. He said "Aye, where y'all from?" I said "What?", then he repeated the question, and Kel responded "The City." The guy nodded his head and said "Ok, 'cuz this my hood!" Me and Kel looked at each other and kept walking. We didn't like to start trouble, but if it came our way, we had no problem handling it. We knew that guy was eventually going to get dealt with.

A couple days later, two guys pulled up to H.O.W. and asked to speak to us. Kel grabbed a gun and asked me to come talk to these guys with him. In a nutshell, the guys told us that they heard we were from The City, and that we were "about that life." That's a common saying in Miami, meaning about that *City* life, since The City represented the most ruthless and dangerous way of life. These guys told us that they were born and raised in The Grove and were down to form some sort of alliance with us, in case someone disrespected us or in case we needed guns or anything else. That was the level of respect that being from The City carried. They also mentioned we were causing friction with the local street gangs and they heard there was a rivalry stirring up. We asked them about the guy who approached us the other day, and they told us he was a wannabe gangster, looking to prove himself. We went back to work, but not before agreeing to meet those guys again on our off day.

That first meeting turned into two, and the second meeting turned into a third, and before we knew it, we were hanging out with those guys almost every day. To the point where we started to call ourselves Street Ridaz (as in "riders"). We were even able to get them jobs at H.O.W., something they've been trying to do for months. We would work during the day, and then go to one of our houses and plot on how we were gonna get rich! We studied movies like *State Property*, *Paid In Full*, *Killa Season*, and *The Life of Rayful Edmond* on the daily. We used these movies as blueprints to build our empire. But little did we know that, what we tune into, we turn into.

Those movies, coupled with listening to gangster rap music like Dipset, Young Jeezy, and T.I. among others, turned us into savages. We were really trying to live out what our minds were consuming. One day after watching one of these movies, the guys told us about the neighborhood weed supplier, he was the "plug" for almost everyone who sold drugs in The Grove. He lived in Coral Gables, one of the more affluent cities in South Florida. He was able to stay low key since his parents had money, and just sell drugs while going to the University Of Miami. They told us they could call him and pretend to place an order, and then we could show up and rob him. It was a sweet lick. A "lick" is what we would call an opportunity for easy money. Whether you had to hustle for it, or simply jacked it.

At this point, Kel and I always carried our guns with us so we were ready to go. They made the phone call and the guy said to meet him at the gas station down the street from his house in 45 minutes. When we pulled up to the gas station, the connect called and said he was two minutes away. He then instructed us to get in his car, so that there would be no funny business. That messed up our original plan of robbing him at the gas station. We agreed, so that we wouldn't raise any red flags. What he didn't know was that he made things much worse for him. When we got in the car, he told us he was taking us to his house to get the "work." Within 30 seconds I put him in a chokehold and told him not to panic. Kel pulled out a sawed off 16 gauge shotgun he had stashed in his jeans, and put it to his head. My other friend had a handgun and told him to drive smoothly the rest of the way. When we pulled in the driveway, he said he was willing to give up everything, as long as we didn't make a scene and wake up his mom. As we walked him to his door, we noticed a police car across the street. His neighbor was a cop. We didn't care, we were in too deep by now, and we were willing to risk it all. When he opened his room door, his girlfriend was asleep. It was past midnight. When we hit the light, she woke up and started crying immediately. So I grabbed a pillow, threw it over her head, pulled my gun out and said "If you don't shut up, I'm gonna blow your head off!" It was as if watching all those movies made it second nature for me to act in this manner. He begged her to be quiet, and told her it'll all be over soon. Kel shoved him against the safe, and told him to open it up. He did. I grabbed two pillowcases and we filled them with cash, drugs, and weapons. We wiped him clean. As we left, we told him if he attempted to follow us, we would make sure he never saw his mom again.

When we got to the house, we emptied the pillowcases and started to divide the money amongst ourselves. We "hit a lick" for a few thousand in cash, a couple of guns, and six pounds of Crip (weed). Then we realized that we forgot the coke, the order we had originally placed to lure him out. We thought of going back. But we spared him this time.

The next day, everyone and their mama knew that we hit a lick on the plug. The fact that we hit the lick barefaced made them draw one of two conclusions; we were either crazy, or just didn't give a damn. The answer was clearly both. Two days later, the plug showed up to H.O.W. to pick up his food. By that time, we were basically running the entire restaurant. He stared us down with rancor. Kel looked at him and said, "You got a problem?" Then proceeded to spit in his food, just for having the audacity to come to our place of work. How dare he? He left, and we never heard from him again.

That lick, led to another, and another, and another. Kel and I developed such a reputation for hitting licks, that whenever a crime happened in The City, the streets echoed our names. Things got so heated that we started to bring negative attention to H.O.W., to the point where Kel and I got jumped by 15 guys outside of work one day. When that happened, we went home, hopped in the Chevy, and told Kel's oldest brother what they did to us. As expected, he grabbed an AK-47 out of the closet and got in the car with us. He told us to take him where they hung out at and that he was going to teach them a lesson. When we pulled up to their block, there were kids playing outside, but Kel's brother didn't care; the guys that jumped us were also there. He got out of the car with the barrel of the gun first, and everyone scattered like roaches. We chased them down, but then we heard sirens, so we left the scene and everyone unharmed.

When we got home later that day, there were cop cars surrounding our house, and everyone from the projects was outside. The cops were interviewing our mom, Ms. Patricia. I told Kel we had a good run, and I would see him on the other side of the concrete jungle, as I assumed we were going down. When we walked up to the cops, our enemies started to point the finger at us, saying things like, "Angel had the AK!" or "No, it was Kel!" We both stayed quiet in denial, as they had no proof. Truth is, Kel's brother got out of the car and told us to stay in. He's the one who had the AK-47, and he never came back with us. But the crowd couldn't get their story straight, and it was their word against ours. So, the cops decided to give us a stay-away order from our rivals. We accepted it and went home.

The next day, when we got to work, Mr. Muhammad pulled me and Kel aside and told us we were no longer employed at his establishment. In disbelief, we argued with him that it wasn't our fault that the beef had escalated so much. He then paused and then wisely said, "Look guys, it's nothing personal. I like you, but war just isn't good for business. I'm sorry, but I have to let you go." I'll never forget that lesson.

Mr. Muhammad was a wise man, which explained his success. He taught us many valuable lessons while we worked there. Things like, "If you work like a slave, you will live like a king." Or "You don't get a second chance at a first impression." And "Shoot for the moon, and if you miss, you will still land amongst the stars." I recall one night, at closing, he was talking to us about a raise, and he looked down on the floor and saw three pennies. He asked us to step back, picked up the change, and told us he would turn them into thousands. His mindset was just built differently.

Kel and I departed from House Of Wings, but we kept our heads high. We couldn't tell our mom, Ms. Patricia, that we lost our jobs over some beef. Our mindsets were Get Down Or Lay Down, a motto we picked up from one of the movies we used to watch. Therefore, we had no choice but to go full time to the streets and do what we did best: rob.

See, the thing is, we weren't just robbing any regular civilian or random people on the streets. We learned that the hard way, when we robbed a pizza delivery man, and when I grabbed him by the shirt and put the gun to his head, he said "Please don't shoot me, I have a family. I only work for tips." We only came up on like $60.00. And Kel and I decided that we didn't want to do that anymore; it didn't feel right. Plus, it was a waste of time. And snatching purses just wasn't our style. We focused on robbing kingpins, drug dealers, and plugs aka the connects of the drug dealers. We once set up a drug lord from Opa-locka, the city next to Miami, that was also notorious for its drug activity and violent crimes. Kel's older brother orchestrated the lick, since he had conducted business with that drug lord in the past. He told him he had a kilo of cocaine fresh from the Bahamas, for $25,000. He told him he could meet within two hours and to come alone. He pretended to have the brick inside of a shoebox, but the box had nothing but a scale in it. As soon as he tried to open the box, I ran up behind him and put him in a rear naked choke, and Kel put the gun to his head. We grabbed his gun, his keys, and of course the bag of money. Later that day, we found out he put a $10,000 bounty on each of our heads. No one ever cashed that check.

We would also hit large grocery chains. We usually knew someone working on the inside, and they would let us know when the morning delivery was happening. We would then show up, kidnap the manager (our inside man), and tell him to take us to the safe and empty it out. We would then meet up later and give him his cut. Then we'd plan for the next location.

Occasionally, we would also rob celebrities. Rappers to be specific. Since Keith was still rapping throughout the entire time, we knew of certain studios where these rappers would come to record. There was a time that Kel and I went months without hitting a lick, and we were really struggling. Our cell phone bill was past due, and we hadn't given our mom any money for the rent. There was a drought, and we weren't getting any leads on any licks, and we were tired of waiting. We had no gas, so we called a friend up to be the driver, and told him we'd give him a cut. After 6 hours of waiting outside the studio house, he couldn't take it and changed his mind and took us home. The next day, still determined to hit this lick, Kel and I took Kel's car on E with the gas light showing. Then the waiting game began. Or as we called it, "lurking" — when you're patiently waiting on someone to slip up.

After 6 hours of lurking, dressed in all black with gloves and ski masks (which we rarely wore since we did most of our licks barefaced), the rapper/producer finally came outside talking on the phone. It was around 3 a.m., and he had a beer in his hand. Just as we expected, he was wearing his $100k diamond watch, and his 20 karat diamond chain. He approached us slowly since he didn't recognize the car. He couldn't see inside; the windows were tinted and humid from us breathing in the car for 6 hours straight. As soon as he got about 2-3 feet from the passenger door, Kel and I counted,

"1-2-3-GO!" We popped the door open, and our target's eyes opened wide as if he'd seen The Devil. He immediately dropped the beer, shattering on impact with the concrete, then turned around and screamed for help. But then he slipped and fell. Kel went to pistol whip him and tell him to shut up, but he had his finger on the trigger and accidentally shot him in the arm simultaneously. We both instantly turned away, but I immediately remembered how long we had been waiting, and how bad we were doing financially. So I went back and snatched the chain off his neck, then hopped in the car. We were in an upper middle-class neighborhood, so we quickly heard sirens everywhere. The cops started setting up a perimeter, but since this wasn't our first rodeo, we slipped by the cop right before he blocked the streets. We made it home safe and sound.

The next morning, we turn on the news, and it's all over the local channels. But we didn't care. We paid our rent and cell phones 3 months in advance after selling the chain to a local diamond broker.

There's always a way to hustle in the hood. Whether it was bank fraud, which later came back to bite us as entrepreneurs, or selling drugs, which ended up staining our records, Kel and I always found a way to make money. But hitting licks was our forte. Truth be told, if I were to go over every detail of all the robberies we did, it would take up the rest of the chapters in this book, and I'd still need to write a sequel. No joke.

One day, our mom, Ms. Patricia, came up to us and acknowledged the fact that we were getting money and helping out around the house. Then, she suggested that we really considered going back to school and graduating. Initially, I saw no point and didn't want to engage in the conversation. But she got closer to me and said; "Baby, listen here. You always finish what you start, no matter what." Though that message resonated with me, I still didn't want to entertain the thought of going back to school. So, I walked out the back door, in deep thought. Kel followed behind me and said, "Fool, maybe it's not a bad idea. Think about it! Why did we really drop out of school in the first place? Because of the lack of clothes and money. Now we have those things! So imagine what we could do if we went back with the type of clothes we have now and the kind of money that we're steady getting?" I just stood silent. Then he said "Think about all the girls we can get." And we both busted out laughing. I told him "Look, let's make a deal. If I don't go back to boxing by the end of this summer, then I'll enrol in school and finish it." He said "Deal," we shook hands, and that was that.

About three months passed by, and I was so focused on getting money that I didn't go back to the gym. Next thing I knew, school was back in session. And since I'm a man of my word, Kel and I enrolled in an alternative school called ACE Academy as a junior and senior in high school.

COMEBACK SEASON

Commitment Is Doing What You Said You Would Do, Long After the Mood You'd Said It in Has Left You

ACE Academy was a fairly small alternative school with about 120 students. Most kids there had either gotten kicked out of their home school for fighting, expelled for drug use or distribution, or simply needed a much smaller classroom size so they could focus on improving their GPA scores. Nevertheless, it served its purpose for what I needed to do, which was to get my high school diploma.

As soon as Kel and I walked in the lunchroom, our aura stood out like a sore thumb. The girls instantly gravitated towards us, and the guys, well, you know they were hatin'.

Once people found out we were from The City, they knew not to play with us. Kel and I had, how can I say this, exquisite taste. We would spend most of our money on clothes. Coming from where we came from, it was our duty to stunt as hard as we could, every chance we got. We wore custom sneakers and made sure our laces matched our fitted hats. We had touch screen cell phones when most students still had flip phones. We had tattoos, gold grills, and even took our guns to school from time to time, just in case.

During lunch one day, Kel and I decided to buy all the pizza boxes from the lunch ladies, so that only our crew, Street Ridaz, and some of the girls could eat. We had other students coming to our table, asking to buy a slice from us. We monopolized the lunchroom at least once a week, just to let it be known who was in charge, and establish our authority. And all the girls were loving it, and the guys hated us or tried to be down with us. I remember one girl came up to me during lunch and said to me, "Man, you're like a god in this school." I laughed and responded, "Naw, you just like my swag."

Kel and I still did our thing every time a good lick came our way, so the money kept flowing in. But eventually, we got bored with school, and Kel dropped out again. As tempted as I was, I was committed to finishing this time. And I did just that, and actually graduated with straight As. And as a side, I also ended up winning best dressed, most photogenic, and most attractive. But no one voted me most likely to succeed.

During graduation, which I was reluctant to attend, no one showed up for me. For whatever reason, people seemed to be tied up that day. It was a bittersweet moment, but I was glad I was done with school.

That same level of commitment got me back in the boxing gym. I got in top shape and turned pro. My first fight was about six months after I graduated from school. I invited a few of the teachers I was close with, and the rest got to watch my pro debut on TV. After breaking the guy's nose in the first round and dropping him twice, I knew this win was a great start to my career. Afterwards, my coach walked up to me in the locker room and said "Well done son, this is just the beginning!" He then handed me my check for my first bout, which was only $600. I was devastated. After almost 6 months of hard training, waking up at 5 a.m. to run 4 miles, I just got $600. I could hit a lick in 60 seconds and make $5,000! My coach saw the look of disappointment on my face, and told me to keep the whole thing; he didn't care about his 30% cut for being my trainer/manager. In that moment I realized how missing the Olympic Trials had truly impacted the trajectory of my career and my financial future. I decided to take another break from boxing, and go back to the streets.

One day, Kel and I were sitting in the living room, listening to one of Keith's mixtapes. Out of nowhere, Kel said we should start rapping. He convinced me that we had the image, the street cred, and with Keith as a musical coach, we would blow up in the industry. So we decided to change our name from Street Ridaz, to J.B.M. (Jack Boy Mafia). A jack boy is basically another word for robber. We now had a different motive for hitting licks: they were an investment in our rap career. We would hit licks and get more tattoos. Hit a lick and invest in our MySpace page. Hit a lick to pay for studio time and some of the biggest features in Miami at the time. Hit a lick, and this was our favorite, and go to the mall. Kel and I developed a fetish for designer clothes. We would go to Bal Harbour, thinking we were celebrities, and blow tens of thousands of dollars at Saks Fifth Avenue, Gucci, and Nordstrom. We became regulars, to the point where the salesclerks addressed us by name. Due to lack of guidance and being badly influenced by other rappers in the game, it would be years until we realized that we were spending money on liabilities, instead of investing in assets.

During that time period, Kel and I easily spent over a quarter of a million dollars on clothes. Not to mention the photoshoot for our album cover, for which we were dipped in Gucci from head to toe, wearing $5k outfits. In retrospect, I realize how misguided we were, thinking this is the way to make it in the rap game. You know, the *fake it 'til you make it* mentality. But I don't regret anything, those were some of the best years of our lives.

I took on the stage name Tyrant a.k.a. Mr. Untouchable, after being inspired by watching a documentary on Nicky Barnes, the Harlem Heroin Kingpin. Plus, the name fit for whenever I decided to go back to boxing, since I was quick and hard to hit. Kel went by the name of Renegade, which fit his personality and character. In no time, the streets adapted our new aliases, and we did everything in our power to prove to the streets that we really lived up to what we rapped about.

Now don't get it twisted, living that life did come with consequences. Kel and I had our fair share of encounters with the law. After multiple occasions, Kel even ended up serving time in prison for selling to an undercover detective. My first time getting locked up, I was only 18. I was on my way to hit a lick and got pulled over. The cop illegally searched the vehicle and found a gun in the glove compartment. I ended up going to trial and losing. The state offered 3 years in prison and 3 years' probation. Luckily, the judge had common sense and could tell that the cop was lying about how the whole thing went down. So he gave me credit time served for it being my first offense.

I remember like it was yesterday, getting out of jail for the first time. I was starving that morning, since I hadn't eaten in jail for a couple of days because of how nasty their food tasted. So I decided to stop by a McDonalds near my house, which was close to the high school I had dropped out of a few months prior. There, I ran into my Language Arts teacher, Mr. Williams. He immediately walked up to me and asked me what was going on and why I had dropped out so close to graduation. I told him I had gotten kicked out of my house, and I had a lot going on. I also let him know that I had just gotten out of jail about an hour from running into him. He looked at me in disappointment, and told me "Angel, get your shit together". Mr. Williams believed in me, just like he did all his students, maybe even a little more than most students. He truly cared about my well being and just didn't want to be reading about me in the local newpaper's *WANTED* section, or even worse, the *OBITUARY* section.

Somehow, every time we got locked up, it had nothing to do with armed robbery; it was always illegal possession of a firearm or narcotics possession with intent to distribute. One time, we even got arrested for arson, but the charges were dropped due to witnesses changing their minds for whatever reason. Jail definitely isn't a place for someone with as much ambition as us, that's for sure!

Having Keith as a rap mentor took things to a whole other level. He'd make us sleep over at his place on the weekends and force us to write music so that we could get better. If we wanted to eat, we had to first write a verse. If we wanted to sleep, we had to first write a verse. Before we even got to brush our teeth, we had to write a verse. This intense level of writing helped us excel amongst our peers, which saved us from embarrassment when performing for other people or simply rapping in a cypher. Those weekends were critical to our lyricism and delivery. It's because of the writing skills he taught me that I am able to write this book today. So always remember, sometimes the present may not make sense, but it always does in the future.

TOUCHED

When a Defining Moment Comes Along, Either You Define The Moment, or The Moment Defines You!

All in all, Kel and I really took our rap career seriously. We even got our nicknames tatted on our necks, that's how far gone we were. But deep down inside, no matter how much we pretended to believe we would make it, we both knew Keith was the golden ticket. So Kel and I decided to put our money where our mouth was, and invest in the printing of his mixtape. After hitting a lick and coming up on roughly $10,000 we took half of it and surprised Keith with a few thousand copies of his physical album, ready for distribution in the streets. He was ecstatic, as we expected, and vowed that our investment wouldn't be in vain.

We were our own little street team, and we would divide and conquer, as we drove all over South Florida, passing out CDs to everyone we knew was a fan, and anyone in a position of power that could potentially get it in the right hands to make him blow up. Occasionally, we would stop by some of the most popular restaurants and corner stores in Miami, and just drop a stack of CDs by the register. Our goal wasn't to sell it for profit, but to make sure everyone was bumping his latest mixtape, Welcome To Kolumbine.

One Sunday afternoon, one of my good friends at the time and a big fan of Keith's, called me up and told me "Let's go pass out some copies," since he knew of some people that had been inquiring about it over the past week. I told him I'd be at his house in 30 minutes to pick him up, so that we could go around delivering CDs for about an hour or so. I remember it like yesterday, I grabbed my Glock 40, and then I thought to myself, "You know what? It's Sunday, my girl is cooking, and I'm not doing anything but going to pass out these CDs and coming right back. I won't be needing this." Then I kissed my gun and put it under my bed. Believe it or not, this was the first time I left my house without a strap in almost 3 years. In some cases, I used to carry two guns just for the hell of it.

As the hour was coming to an end, the friend I was with told me we had one last stop before I dropped him home. He said he knew of a guy who was a big fan of Keith's, and we had to give him a mixtape. When he gave me the address, I broke out in goosebumps. The drop off location was in the Brown Sub projects, in Liberty City. I could count in one hand how many times I had returned to Brownsville since the house got shot up that day. And most, if not all of those times, were to do drive-by shootings, or robberies and shootouts. Only thing was this time, I didn't have my gun with me. Still, I wasn't overly worried. What were the chances of something going down in broad daylight, at 4 p.m. on a Sunday?

My friend pointed out the parking lot where, to my surprise, I saw about 20 guys gambling at the entrance of the complex. As we drove by them, I made eye contact with a familiar face that I knew from the hood. He was rolling dice, so I paid him no mind and kept driving. I then noticed that the parking lot was one way in, one way out. I came to a stop. My friend then told me that the guy was supposed to be outside waiting, but he was nowhere to be found. As I made a U-turn to leave, my friend pointed out that the guy who was on our left as we were driving into the parking lot, had now moved so that he was once again on our left as we were driving out. He was clearly wanting to be as close to me, the driver, as possible. On top of that, he had his hand in his back pocket, as if he had a gun. I looked at my friend and said, "He better not try anything, or he will die tonight!" I approached the exit, there was a speed bump that caused me to almost come to a complete stop. When I slowed down and looked to my left, there he was, grilling me with his gold teeth about two feet away from my door. I made eye contact once again and then turned away as I stepped on the accelerator. Within seconds, all I heard was gunshots going off. Next thing I know, I felt my body jerk. I felt as if I was electrocuted at first, so I swerved the steering wheel almost crashing into a pole. Shots were still ringing. I managed to gain control of the vehicle as I screamed to my friend, "I'm hit! I'm hit!"

The bullet had gone through the car door, through the seat, my pants and shoes, and hit me in my Achilles tendon on my left foot. I immediately reached for my hip, where I usually kept my gun, but it wasn't there. I got caught slippin'. I grabbed my phone and called Kel. I told him who shot me and told him to handle that for me. Then I hung up and started to drive towards the hospital. I soon noticed I was losing too much blood, so I pulled over and told my friend to take the wheel.

Here's where it gets crazy. My friend was a super chill dude. All he did was go to work and go home to smoke weed. He was my neighbor when I lived in Brown Sub, and it was him that actually introduced me to Kel. He was so chill, that he always used to wear slides everywhere he went. But on this day, for some odd reason, he tells me he needs to turn around, and go home to put on some shoes. Then he proceeds to drive home, the opposite way of the hospital. When he got there, he ran in the house, and after a minute, his whole family came out to the car to ask me what had happened. I couldn't believe this was happening. They knew how me and Kel got down, so they begged me not to kill the guy who shot me. I couldn't make any promises.

When we finally made it to Jackson Memorial Hospital, the same hospital I was born in, they rushed me to the emergency room. As I laid in bed, waiting for a doctor, a cop walks up and arrests me. They told me it was protocol, until they investigated, who, what, when, and where the shooting happened. I told them I didn't know who shot me, since I got hit from the backside. I maintained the "No Snitching" code of the streets and remained silent. Plus, I wanted to take matters into my own hands. They had no choice but to let me go. After 6 hours, the doctors finally came back with the X-ray results. They told me I was lucky, no bones were broken, no veins hit, and no ligaments were torn. They advised me to leave the bullet in my leg, because if I decided to extract it, they would have to chop off 3-4 inches of the bone in my ankle. So, I left the bullet inside my foot, and walked out on crutches. Their only suggestion was that if I chose to go back to boxing, to give it at least a year to fully heal.

When I made it to the car, all I was thinking about was how I was going to explain to my girl that I got her car shot up. There were about 8 bullet holes in the car. Detectives were there taking samples. They told me one bullet hit my seat, just 2 inches away from my spine. I was blessed not to be paralyzed. One cop saw the tattoo on my neck and said "Mr. Untouchable! Looks like you got touched today" then laughed and walked away. My girl was already waiting for me by the car. She wasn't tripping, she was just glad I was OK. As she drove my friend back home that night, he got a phone call from someone in the hood, saying that the guy who shot me was dead.

The next day, the pain really hit me. I had lost so much blood, I was too weak to even stand up. My girl, with whom I had been living with for about six months, was a CNA, studying to be an RN. She took care of me the entire time of my recovery. That truly made me fall in love with her, and made me want to slow down with the streets. Ultimately, she wanted me to go to school, get a good job, and for us to live happily ever after. But I still had big dreams of being rich and famous as a rapper or a boxer, whichever came first. Shortly after my recovery, she broke up with me and I went back to the streets doing what I did best, hitting licks. I temporarily moved back with Kel and Ms. Patricia. I felt as if I had hit rock bottom.

Later on, I found out that the guy who shot me was still alive. They started a rumor that he was dead in order to save his life. But he had just gone into hiding. Every morning I would wake up angry and wanting revenge. I knew where the guy was, he wasn't hard to find, I just didn't want to get caught. I felt disrespected. How would the street feel about me if I let this slide? It would ruin my street cred and my reputation as a rap artist. I'd spend at least an hour a day just plotting and planning. Until one night I was outside scheming on my next move, and I looked up at the sky, and I saw a shooting star. I immediately closed my eyes and started praying. I said "God, why is it that every time I feel that I'm on top of the world, you always bring me back down and I end up hitting rock bottom? What am I doing wrong? Please just give me a sign." Then I walked in the house and went to sleep.

The next morning, I picked up my phone, and saw a text from my coach: *MATHEW* 6: 14-15 "For if you forgive other people when they sin against you, your heavenly father will also forgive you. But if you do not forgive others their sins, your father will not forgive your sins." See, over the past five years, my coach had been texting me a verse from the bible every single day. Though I was half asleep, I knew this was the sign that I had asked for the night before. I would be a fool to ignore it. There were two people I held a grudge for and didn't want to forgive; the guy who shot me, and my mom for kicking me out and costing me my chance at the Olympics. Right then and there, I told myself deep inside, I forgive that guy and will let God take care of him. Then I picked up the phone, called my mom, and asked her if I could move back in. It had been over 5 years. She said "Of course."

Later in life I learned from one of my mentors that holding a grudge is like drinking poison and expecting the other person to die.

ROCK DID IT, AGAIN!

My Introduction to Business

When I moved back in with my mom, my little brother and sister still lived there. I had been in contact with my little brother throughout the years, so he knew exactly what I was about and what kind of stuff I was into. He was a party animal, so knowing I was just getting over a breakup, he invited me to the club for the first few weekends. It's probably the only time in my life I went to a club, aside from rap performances here and there, but he claimed it would help speed up the healing process. I guess it did help.

A few weeks after moving in, my brother brought an idea to my attention. He told me that the fall semester at college was starting soon, and I should really consider enrolling. He told me, since the street life wasn't going as planned, maybe college would open up doors for different opportunities. It was hard to admit, but he was right. After all those years of running the streets, I had nothing to show for it but some designer clothes and shoes. I had tried robbing, selling drugs, and every illegal way there was to get rich. I felt like a failure, so I was open to his idea. I even tried going back to boxing, but when I attempted to run 4 miles a day for my endurance training, my foot clearly hadn't fully healed yet. I guess my teachers were right from the beginning; the only way to become successful was to go to college and get a good job.

I started going to school and decided to leave the streets behind. I was lucky to make it out alive. After all, Kel was already serving time on those drug charges I mentioned before. So I was willing and open to change. We've all heard the cliché, the definition of insanity is doing the same thing over and over and expecting a different result. When it comes to change, the first step is awareness. And the second step is acceptance. I was aware of the decisions I had made up to that point, and accepted the fact I needed to be humble and follow in the footsteps of my younger brother. Who, despite his tendency to party and drink, at least had a solid plan as to what he wanted to do.

Within a couple of months of starting college, things were going pretty well. I was getting straight As in all my general education courses. I was making new friends and connections. I even found me a new girlfriend who worked at a bank, and she was helping me get my life in order. She knew of my past, but she was into that "bad boy" persona. We met at the downtown campus I was attending, when I had mistaken her for a girl I met at the club a few weeks prior. She helped me get back on my feet, not just emotionally, but financially.

One morning, my brother and I were walking to our next class, when he spotted a flyer on the bulletin board. Full of enthusiasm, he grabbed that piece of paper. When I asked what it was, he said, "A great opportunity for you!" The flyer was a Disney College Recruitment seminar they were having on campus the following week. He explained to me that this was a way for me to get a job and how he'd worked there the year before. See, due to my record, finding employment was difficult at the time. He told me that Disney World in Orlando, FL, had a college program where active college students could intern. Their motto was; you can live, learn, and earn, all at Disney University. I had to admit it; the deal sounded pretty sweet. It was an 8-month internship, in which they provided boarding, employment, and schooling. All I had to do was get accepted.

We went to the computer lab the same day, and he helped me fill out and submit my application. Then, I went to praying, hoping, and wishing they would bypass my record. They were only paying $7.25/hr, but that was more than the $0.00/hr I was getting at the time. After weeks of anticipation, I got the email stating that I had been accepted to the Disney

College Program, and was expected to arrive in Orlando in about 8 weeks. I was excited, but my girlfriend didn't take it very well. But I vowed to come back and visit her every month since I would only be about three hours away.

Disney World had over 60,000 employees at the time, and 12,000 of them were part of the college internship. Out of those 12,000, 8,000 were domestic students, and 4,000 were international exchange students. This diversity would end up causing me quite a culture shock later on. The students were all housed in 4 different apartment complexes. And they had a bus system that transported us back and forth from the homes to the parks. Their classrooms were also inside the complexes, making it easy for us to attend and stay on top of our education.

The day we arrived, we went straight to orientation. My brother and sister also applied and got accepted, and I was glad I wasn't alone. Overall, I was truly grateful to be far away from Miami. The change of scenery was most definitely needed. After hours of orientation, they had a meet-and-greet with food and drinks. This is where I realized how my environment had taken its toll on my life. I had never seen so many happy people in one place. Especially coming from the Brown Sub projects. I mean they don't call it the happiest place on earth for no reason. Even the music was happy — they were playing pop songs; songs that were much different from the gangster music I knew by heart. When it was over, I felt overwhelmed and relieved at the same time.

You see, growing up in Liberty City, all I was used to was seeing drug use, violence, and aggression everywhere. If you were a guy, the choices were, you either become a dope boy, or a robber (and we all know which route I chose). And if you were a girl, it was normal to get pregnant before finishing high school, drop out, and then become a stripper after the baby was born. It was like it was all predetermined. The odds of making it as a pro athlete, for example, were slim to none. And coming from an environment like that, to this, let's just say all eyes were on me at all times, from day one. I mean I looked, walked, and talked like a rapper. From the gold teeth in my mouth, to the use of the word "fool" every other sentence, people were mind boggled that I was now one of them.

The next morning, I woke up and checked my email to see where I'd been assigned to work, as my sister and brother both got their occupation. To my surprise, I found a different type of email. It was from Disney's private internal compliance department. The email basically read that they had no idea how I had made it this far in their process given my background. They instructed me to pack all my belongings and wait for their phone call so that I may be escorted off the premises. I was disheartened and devastated. Just when I was starting to have hope for a better future.

When I finally got the call, it was a sweet older woman. She told me that she had been looking over my case all day, and after reviewing it, she concluded that if I had made it this far in their process, God had to had been on my side. She then told me that if I wanted to work for them, I would have to find all the transcripts for my trial with the gun charge and submit them to her. Not only that, but I would have to write an essay explaining every single offense I had on my record — why it happened, and why it was dismissed — as well as why they should consider allowing me to work there and why I had changed my life. The whole process took a couple of weeks, during which I was basically on house arrest and wasn't allowed to leave my apartment at all. Once I had completed everything, the lady in charge of my case was so pleased with my diligence and story, that she asked me to come meet her at her office when and if I completed my internship so that she could simply give me a hug. She told me she had never seen a case like mine and hoped that I didn't take the opportunity for granted. She said she was proud of me and my persistence, and I was hired effective immediately.

During the entire program, I had to wear a turtleneck, even when the weather was over 100 degrees, due to their "no visible tattoo" policy. Once the program was over, I went to the lady's office to give her a hug, as per her request. It was a secret location only the top Disney execs get to go to. I brought a thank-you card with me just because I was grateful to get a second chance. But when I got to the reception, they told me that that lady didn't exist, and that they had no idea who I was talking about, and to please leave the building immediately... It must've been God all along.

About a month before my internship was over, I had asked God for another sign, since I wasn't sure what my next step should be. I hadn't saved up as much money as I was planning to when I first came there. Not to mention, the frequent weekend trips to Miami to visit my girl weren't cheap, especially since I was only making minimum wage. Two days later, my mom called me, telling me she was in Alaska working, and that they were looking for people to work there for a few months. I took that as my sign and booked my flight to Alaska for the same day my program ended.

When I landed in Alaska, it was unlike anything I had ever seen. 'Til this day, I've been to about 40 states, and Alaska is by far the most beautiful state I have ever traveled to. It was the perfect place for me to focus and stack my money. Plus, it was far enough so that I couldn't just up and leave to spend the weekend in Miami. This put a strain on my relationship with my girl. I really loved her, but she wasn't having it. She was fed up with all the long-distance B.S. I was putting her through. I came back a few months after, but it was too late. The distance had taken its toll on our relationship, and she left me. Once again, I was single and heartbroken.

Back in Miami, I had a few thousand dollars to my name. Kel had gotten out by now. So between him, my little brother and me, we decided to rent a house and move in together. Kel knew a girl he was talking to, and her uncle was in real estate and he had a house for rent within our budget. The only thing was, it was located in Little Haiti. We moved in and started doing renovations. Although, after the down payment, we put carpet in the entire house and then I ran out of money. We had no furniture; we were sleeping on the floor. And Kel was the only one working, a part time job doing door to door sales. Once again, I was lost and felt like I hit rock bottom.

I started thinking, maybe I should go back to the streets. Then it hit me! Out of nowhere I remembered, Rocky had wished me happy birthday on Facebook a few weeks earlier and had asked me to give him a call. It had been over 10 years since I last spoke to him. He had stopped boxing after developing chronic bronchitis and became a celebrity barber. We had been Facebook friends for years, but never even spoke. I had been watching everything he was doing, and it seemed like he was successful. I thought to myself, if someone can help me get out of my situation and move forward, then it's Rocky!

It was a Friday night, approximately 9 p.m.. I nervously called Rocky, not knowing what to expect, but I was desperate for a change. He answered on the first ring! I said, "It's Angel, from the boxing gym!" He was excited to hear from me but told me he was about to walk into a meeting, so he couldn't talk but he would text me. We went back and forth texting for about 30 minutes. He asked me if I was still boxing, I told him no, that I had gotten shot, and that I had just gotten out of jail not too long ago. I explained to him that I was struggling and was looking for work. He asked me if I had a car, I told him no. He then asked me what I was doing Saturday morning at 9 a.m.. I said, "Nothing, why?" Then he said, "Be dressed in business attire sharp tomorrow morning at 8 a.m.. I'll send someone to pick you up. We're going to travel the world and make a lot of money!" He then explained he was working with a company and was going to put in a good word with the people at the top. Rocky was talking my language. I always had dreams of being rich and traveling the world. I ran in the room and told my brothers where I was invited to, then I set my alarm, got my clothes ready, and went to sleep.

LIGHTS, CAMERA, ACTION!!!

Once the Mind Is Stretched by an Idea or Thought, It Will Never Go Back to Its Original Dimensions

The next morning, I threw on an outfit that I thought was professional yet looked like I had money. After all, you don't get a second chance to make a first impression. I got a phone call from a young lady, stating she was outside waiting for me. I got in and introduced myself; she then started to drive north, about 45 minutes to the Sheraton Suites Hotel. The entire way there she spoke highly of Rocky, as I expected. She barely mentioned anything about where we were going. All she said was that this opportunity was going to change my life. I sure as hell hoped so.

When we arrived, the parking lot was almost full, so it took us a while to find a spot. We walked in the lobby and there were hundreds of people standing in line, waiting for the doors to open. The whole time I was expecting a one-on-one interview, but now I thought I was going to have to compete with all these people to secure a position. The crowd was really happy and upbeat. Everyone was greeting each other with hugs and kisses. I felt as if I was in a Disney orientation all over again, except this time with adults in suits. I spotted Rocky as he stood out in the crowd, looking sharper than most, as usual. I walked up to him, shook his hand and gave him a hug. Then I immediately asked him who all these people were. He told me not to mind them, and to just follow him. We skipped the line, and I sat next to him. He then told me to pay attention, and to take notes on the pad he asked me to bring. Then the music came on, the crowd stood up, and the first speaker hit the stage.

Later on, I realized I was sitting in a Business Opportunity Meeting for one of the top network marketing companies in the globe. I had never heard of this industry, let alone this company. They were the world's largest direct seller of telecom, energy, and other essential services, with revenues surpassing $500 million annually. And they had the awards and documentation to back it up. Their business model was customer acquisition through relationship and referral-based marketing. The direct selling industry is one of the largest industries in the world, rivaling real estate, when it comes to creating the most millionaires and billionaires.

The first presenter was cool, but when he introduced the second speaker, I was mind-blown by his high energy levels and speaking skills. He was a 25-year-old, half Filipino half Puerto Rican gentleman. He was dressed in a custom tailored suit, with alligator Louis Vuitton shoes. He wore a Breitling timepiece, with diamonds around the bezel. His haircut was razor sharp, like something out of a magazine. His tie matched with his socks, which barely showed at the cuff of his pants. He was so charismatic as he masterfully extracted laughs from the crowd, while simultaneously dropping gems consistently. In my eyes, he was the epitome of success.

Throughout his entire presentation, he would share thought-provoking quotes like, "J.O.B. stands for Just Over Broke." He said "Most people are poor minded, P.O.O.R. meaning Passing Over Opportunities Repeatedly." He taught us some wealth principles such as *leverage* and *residual income*, things they didn't teach me in school. He talked about change and taking action, and left us with this, "Your level of thinking has gotten you to where you are currently at right now. And if you're not happy where you're at financially in life, you need to stop thinking and start acting! For things to change in your life, *you* must change! It's choice, not chance that determines your destiny!" I'm not sure what was more impressive; the fact that he was a college dropout yet an eloquent businessman, or the fact that he was making more in one month than most people earned all year. Either way, when the seminar was over, I didn't remember any of the details, I just remembered how I felt. I felt great, empowered, and hopeful! The only issue was, I didn't have the money to get started.

It was $500 to buy an online store with a franchise-like model. I could then become an independent sales rep, and by using their proven system I could then advance to the different level ranks and reach the maximum levels of compensation. Not gonna lie, the concept seemed flawless; getting paid when people paid their bills, a complete no brainer. Not to mention, there were people in the meeting who looked like me, that were winning and making big money, and transforming their lives, something you don't see very often in the corporate world. But what really got me was the fact that they didn't care about my background. They were only interested in my work ethic. Then I thought to myself, if all else fails, I could always come back and rob the main speaker, so it was a win-win for me.

After the meeting, Rocky pulled me aside, and asked me was I ready to get started? I told him everything sounded great, however, I didn't have any money. I actually had 500 excuses as to why I couldn't get started. I told him,"Look, I'm not a good speaker, I've been hit in the head too many times from boxing. I don't have a job. I don't have a car. I don't have any credibility, I just got out of jail. I don't have a laptop. I don't even have friends, I have enemies! I can't even walk straight, I have a bullet inside of me!" Then he stared at me dead in the eyes and said "You can make excuses or you can make money, but you can't make both." Right then and there, I decided not to let my past control my destiny. Though I lacked many things, one thing I did have was a burning desire to change my life. And I was determined and dedicated to making that happen! I told him as long as he's willing to coach me, I'd do everything he and the presenter told me to do.

I went home that day, and told my brothers I was starting a business, and that they should, too. They asked no questions and were down to do whatever I was doing. I always spoke highly of Rocky to them, so they knew he meant business in everything he did. Then I called my mom and asked her to borrow the $500. When she asked me what it was for and I explained, she was turned off instantly. She told me "Those things don't work" and continued to discourage me over the next 20 minutes. I still got the funds, but she jaded my vision a bit.

I called Rocky as soon as I left her house and told him I had borrowed the money to start. I also informed him that my mom suggested this wasn't a good idea and that I shouldn't invest my money. Then Rocky asked me a set of questions that led to one of my biggest lessons in business. He asked me what my mom did for work. I told him she was currently unemployed. Then he asked me whether I would take medical advice from a mechanic. I said no. Then he asked whether I would take legal advice from someone with no legal background. I responded that, no, of course I wouldn't. He then asked whether I would take advice on how to lose weight from someone who's overweight. I wouldn't. Finally, he said, "So why would you take business advice from someone who's never owned a business?" He told me that if I buy into someone's opinion, I will buy into their lifestyle. And if I wouldn't trade places with them financially, I shouldn't listen to them about investments. Lastly, he suggested I listen to people who had what I wanted, and to do what they did, and I'll end up having what they have.

I felt enlightened. I decided to no longer take constructive criticism from people who've never constructed anything. If I were going to achieve my goal of being rich, I was going to have to only listen to wealthy people. Because listening to poor-minded people would only keep me broke. Rocky then challenged me to go on a mental diet. Something I'd never heard of. Just like our bodies, our mind is cluttered with garbage and toxic, detrimental thoughts. He told me, what we tune into, we turn into. The challenge was to last 30 days, and it consisted of not watching TV and not listening to music. Anytime I felt like watching TV, I had to read a book. Anytime I felt like listening to the radio, I would listen to a personal development audio. He promised me that doing so would cleanse my mind and help me think like an investor instead of a consumer. The first book he suggested was Rich Dad Poor Dad.

Up until this point, I had never read a book in my life. Let alone dabbled in the world of personal growth and development. Rocky taught me that there were two types of education: formal and informal. Formal education would make you a living, but self-education or informal education would make you a fortune. And so I accepted his challenge and dove headfirst into the first book he suggested. I started to learn the difference between *assets* and *liabilities*. That's when I realized that I had been spending all of my money over the past years on nothing but liabilities. To simplify the concept, liabilities are things that take money out of your pocket. Assets are things that put money into your pockets. The book further explained how rich people buy luxuries last, while poor people buy them first. The poor spend their money and invest what's left, if anything at all. While the rich invest first and spend what's left. I felt bamboozled. I had unknowingly and unintentionally developed poor habits.

All of a sudden, I had a flashback moment to when I was working at House of Wings. I remember walking in on my day off, and the manager at the time, Dre, was reading the exact same book that Rocky had just given me. When I inquired what he had been reading so intently, he told me the name of the book and explained to me what it was about. He then suggested that I read the book and that it could potentially change my life. How ignorant and closed-minded I must have been back then. I remember telling him, "Fool, you know street niggas from the hood don't read," and then I laughed and walked away. Thankfully, I was wiser this time around and took Rocky's advice.

The following weekend, Rocky sent the same young lady to pick me up and take me to the event. I showed up at the same time, and sat through the same presentation. After it was done, I asked Rocky, how many of these training sessions did I have to attend? He then countered me with his own question, "How often do you go to work?" I told him every day. So then he said, "Can you come to a training once a week to eventually become financially free? I said, "Yes, sir!" He explained to me that becoming successful was simply mastering the mundane. He then made it click for me by telling me that if I were to treat this like boxing, I would get flat out rich. See, when we used to train, we would go 6 days a week. But on Saturdays, the gym would be damn near empty. When I asked my coach why that was, he told me "Angel, only true champions train on Saturdays." All I had to do was apply that same philosophy. And I would achieve greatness in this arena.

One day after a meeting, Rocky asked me why I was doing this business. I explained to him that I was an up-and-coming rapper and would love it if I could use the income from the business to fund my music career. He then gave me a perspective that changed the game for me. He asked me why I could memorize a song from the radio for free, but not memorize a presentation that could get me rich. The reason he asked me was that one of the conditions I had set for getting involved with the business was that Rocky was never to ask me to speak in front of anyone. That's when he told me that the people in the front of the room always make the most money. So deep down I knew, if I were to ever get to the big money that was available, I was going to have to get comfortable being uncomfortable and do the presentations.

The less I listened to music, the more I realized what it was doing to my mind. I knew that if I was going to drastically change my life, I had to drastically change the way I was thinking. I started to understand that most people were wired for success but programmed for failure. Before I knew it, my language started to change little by little. My vocabulary started to expand, and so did my thoughts. I became addicted to working on myself. I learned that success isn't something you pursue, but it's something you attract by the person you become.

A few months before going to my first business event with Rocky, I had applied and got accepted to another Disney internship for eight months. I had applied as a fallback plan, just in case I wasn't able to find any work in Miami. But when this opportunity arose, I figured that this was the perfect formula for success. I now knew that businesses take time to build, and that this wasn't a get rich quick scheme. So I needed to work full time at a job, and part time on my fortune, until one day, my fortune would surpass my full time income. In business, you have to invest first before you see any results. Whether it's time, energy, or money, a business *requires* investments. So I decided to move to Orlando and use that income to support my side hustle. The new semester was only a couple weeks away, and I was committed to making it worth my time, this time more than last. There was only one little problem, my body started to push out the bullet that was lodged in my leg for two and a half years now.

MURPHY'S LAW

Anything That Can Go Wrong, Will Go Wrong

My foot started to swell up, which kept me from attending a couple of training events. It got to the point where I couldn't walk, and so I went to the hospital to have emergency surgery. I was then discharged on crutches. I knew it was nothing but a minor setback for a major comeback. Just like in boxing, you may get a busted lip, or your eye closed shut, but then you go to your corner, they put some ice on it and send you back out to fight. I had developed a warrior-like mentality from all those years of boxing, so I brought it into the business world with me. And just like that, I was back doing meetings on crutches. My coach would always tell me, boxing is 80% mental and 20% physical — and business was no different.

I vividly recall one of the first private business meetings I held at my house in Little Haiti. I didn't have many friends, so I called up the few ones I did have. I simply told them, come to my house, at a certain time, if you want to make some money. Until then, I hadn't realized how bad my reputation had gotten. My friends showed up, dressed in all black, brought guns, and their ski masks with them. I told them this wasn't that type of money-making meeting. They said they were expecting to plot and hit a lick with me. I told them I was a changed man and wasn't going back to my old ways. They laughed in disbelief; I was dead serious.

They say that if your circle doesn't inspire you, then it's not a circle, it's a cage. Elevation requires separation, but most people are not willing to leave their friends and family behind in order to take their lives to the next level. Not me; I didn't love my friends enough to stay broke with them. *Rich Dad Poor Dad* explained that the bigger our network, the bigger our net worth, something that naturally solidified my decision to grow and elevate my network. We are the combined average of the five people we spend the most time with. Hang out around five baseball players, you're bound to pick up a bat. Hang out with five alcoholics, it's just a matter of time before you pick up a beer. I hung around thugs, so it was no wonder that I was carrying a gun and engaging in obscene activities day in, day out. The same rules apply on the other end of the spectrum; if you hang around five successful people, you're bound to pick up on their habits and become the sixth successful person in your circle.

Right then and there I knew that I needed to make some new friends. Friends that had the same common future, not just the same common past. Disney was the perfect place to start building my network from scratch. There were people from all walks of life and from all different parts of the world. However, I knew that if I was going to be moving away from the support and training system that was in place back home, I was going to have to be extra focused and disciplined. Plus, a wise man once told me, "If you want to make it in life, move away from your hometown. Support doesn't come from familiar faces."

When I first got to Disney, I took a personal vow to never change, and remain the same while I made it to the top. I didn't want any one of my friends I grew up with saying, "He got rich, then he switched" or "He acts different now that he has money." I even kept my gold grill in my mouth while I worked at my job, and while I did presentations for my side business. Then one day I randomly lost them while I was working. I then realized that those grills were truly holding me back and that I'd lost them for a reason. Next time you feel stuck, ask yourself; what are you willing to give up, in order to go up? We all have blind spots, and a lot of the time it takes an outside perspective for us to see what we've been missing. Just like during a boxing match, when your coach may be yelling for you to keep your hands up, even though you feel you *have* them up. It's not until you get hit in the chin that you realize your coach was right. But by then it's too late for most.

I spent about a hundred dollars on ten different books to take with me to Orlando. But not just any books; these were books that were highly recommended from my mentors, and in alignment with my business goals. Not all books are for all people. Therefore, they should be prescribed just like medicine, according to the person's symptoms. My mentor told me that I should always work harder on myself than I worked at my job. So over the next eight months, which was the length of my internship, I committed to doing just that. From the first day I arrived, all I did was go to work, and come home and read. This level of consistency helped sharpen my leadership and communication skills very rapidly. Not only was I beginning to speak differently, but I also started thinking differently. But most importantly, I was communicating differently. Leaving an impact is important, especially in sales. People may not remember what you said, but they will always remember how you made them feel.

I became an avid reader, which is funny because I used to hate reading. Luckily, I didn't hate it more than my desire to win. I also became aware that even though all readers are not leaders, all leaders do read. I was so hungry for success that I would hop on conference calls every other day, just so I could learn the language of my industry. In every industry there is a language. The moment that the expert's words come out of your mouth, their money will go into your bank account. My roommates thought I was crazy, they called me boring. I wouldn't attend any of the parties. I didn't go out to eat. That 30-day mental diet challenge had turned into a lifestyle. They probably thought I was really nuts and obsessed since I rarely even listened to music. I was determined to give it my all and I refused to go back to where I came from.

When the checks started to roll in, I would invest the majority of it in myself and into my business. Knowing that most businesses go out of business within their first two years, I knew that by investing back into myself and my business I would lower the chances of becoming a casualty as an entrepreneur. It was like the more I grew, so did the checks. So that reassured me that I was on the right track. Rocky and I would talk multiple times a day. On one particular day, he asked me whether I had been reading the books he had recommended. I told him "Of course." That's when he gave me the analogy, how business was just like boxing. In boxing, if the coach told you to go to the track and run 4 miles, at 5:00 a.m. every day, he wouldn't actually be there to make sure that you were, in fact, running. But when you got in the ring, it would be obvious from your results whether or not you'd put in the effort. This is why my coach's motto was, "If you cheat, you're only cheating yourself." And I knew that if I wasn't reading daily, Rocky would be able to tell during my presentations. Needless to say, my presenting skills were getting impeccable.

When it comes to your goals and dreams, anybody can be excited in the moment, so long as they have the proper vision casted and in the right environment. Most people can even stay excited for a full month. Some stay excited for 90 days. A few can stay excited and enthusiastic throughout an entire year. But only a true champion will stay excited and motivated until they win. If you want to succeed, it is crucial that you become — and stay — self-disciplined. Self-motivation is key, because you're not always going to feel like doing everything that you need to do on a daily basis in order to attain your goal. Sometimes I would work 60-70 hour weeks, 14 hour shifts, and still came home dedicated to reading for at least twenty minutes a day. I started to master this disciplined lifestyle, and the checks were starting to show it.

My coworkers at Disney would make fun of me. They would say things like, "If you're a businessman why are you working here?" Or, "If you're making so much money with your side business, then why do you work here for minimum wage?" Little did they know that I was there on a mission to expand my network, and making money was my second priority. That's why it's important to have thick skin when going into business for yourself. I had to literally psych myself up daily, by repeating the mantra, "This will be the last job I'll ever have to work in my life." They say the fastest way to kill a big dream is to share it with a small-minded person. I had really big dreams, and it was those daily affirmations that helped turn them into reality. Within a few months, my weekly business checks were exceeding my monthly Disney checks. By the time my internship program was over, I was making more every two weeks from my business, than I made the entire time I stayed at Disney. But you know what they say; what goes up, must come down.

Once a quarter, I was attending business conventions all over North America with some of the most prolific speakers and bestselling authors this world has to offer. During one of the business dinners, one of my mentors said something so profound that it helped me both psychologically and emotionally for long after that night. He said, "Momentum in business will make you look better than you actually are. However, lack of momentum will make you look worse than you actually are. Therefore, never let the wins get to your head, nor the losses get to your heart." At the time, I was experiencing five-figure months, and his words resonated with me. This led me to take full responsibility for all the good, bad, and ugly that happened in my business. The biggest gap in the world is that between knowing and doing. Many people claim to know, but few actually *do* what they know. Ideas are abundant, execution is rare.

After a couple of years of being in business, that $100 worth of books I invested in had given me a 1000 fold return on my money. I started speaking at events and business conventions with tens of thousands of people in attendance. Everyone was interested in knowing how a guy with my type of background was achieving the level of success that I was seeing in such a short period of time. Shortly after speaking at a convention in LA with over 20,000 people, I got a message from a lady in Vancouver B.C., Canada through Facebook, seeking advice and mentorship. Her and her business partner had heard me on stage, and needed help with their business. I started to coach her over the phone on a weekly basis. Eventually we were talking daily, and most importantly, she was taking action on the coaching I was giving her. The following year, she was able to generate multiple six figures through her business, and was featured in *Success Magazine*. When you're doing well for yourself, it is important to help others; not just financially, but with your time and knowledge. It's a fulfilment no amount of money can bring.

Everything was going smooth and steady, until one day I got a call from the company's compliance department. When I answered, they started interrogating me about my little brother. After answering all of their questions, they told me they were permanently deactivating his account, due to some unethical behavior. I couldn't believe it. Next to Kel, my little brother was bringing in the most customers, and making me a lot of money in the process. I was devastated and did everything in my power to reinstate his position, but it was too late. That's when I learned the importance of integrity. Integrity is what you do, when no one else is watching. And how you do anything in life, is how you do everything. He had made some selfish moves in his life and his business, and it affected the entire team negatively. My check was basically cut by 30%.

The fact that my mentor had dealt with a similar situation but was now earning ten times more than me helped me cope with the situation. It was then that I decided to apply what I call *recovery time* in boxing. My coach once taught me after a sparring session that the time it takes you to recover from a hard hit will determine if you come back and win the fight and ultimately become a champion. He told me, "Never let a hit turn into a blow that will end up knocking you out of the fight!" Having this mindset will help you during tough times. You want to get to the point where your emotions don't dictate the level of action you take towards your goals. As one of my mentors would always say, "Your future is more important than your feelings!"

Please understand that when you set big goals, the universe will test you to see how bad you want it. And like I always say, the universe isn't going to punch you on your arm, it's going to kick you in the nuts! It'll hit you where it hurts, and when and where you least expect it. When it rains it pours. That my friend, is Murphy's Law.

Kel and I have always had some sort of mastermind. Whether in the streets or in business, we held each other accountable to our greatest potential. The fact that we were both former athletes, really gave us a healthily competitive type of friendship. We would always do our best to outdo each other. We would try to see who could dress better, who could get the most girls, and of course, who would get rich the fastest. We had the same taste for the finer things in life, so it helped us be on the same page when it came to most things. Then one day we received a call from his sister, with the worst news we had ever gotten. Ms. Patricia, our sweet mother, had come home from the hospital with positive results from her cervical cancer exam. We were heartbroken. Especially Kel — more than anyone in the family, in my opinion. She was his reason *why*. He wouldn't talk about his dreams without mentioning how he was going to take care of her. We tried everything within our resources, from positive affirmations to holistic healing remedies, everything failed. Within months the cancer spread from her cervix to her bones, and finally to her brain.

On November 19, 2013 we didn't lose Ms. Patricia; we gained an angel. That same night, I had to go to a business event. Just as you shouldn't bring your emotions in the ring, you should never bring your feelings in the business field; business is never personal. In life, there are things we can control, and things we can't, and death is one of them. Kel relocated to Atlanta, GA, and started his life over and has since found a new passion and purpose in the film industry.

NO PAIN NO GAIN

If You're Feeling Pain, It's either Because
You're Leaving Your Comfort Zone, or
Because You've Been in It for Too Long

When Kel left Miami, my income was cut down by about 70% compared to what I was used to making the year before. Luckily for me, I had listened to my mentor and began managing my money better, so my overhead wasn't so high. He told me "When your outcome exceeds your income, your upkeep will soon become your downfall." That quote pierced through me, so I did everything in my power to be responsible with my money so that I could stay in business. It wasn't easy by any means, but it was definitely worth it. Which brings me to another lesson from boxing: you could slow down but never stop!

When I first started going to the boxing gym, one of the assistant coaches instructed us to run a mile. After we finished, he asked me whether I had stopped during my run. I told him that I had felt a cramp, and so I had stopped for a minute or two. He told me to do it again. After I returned, he asked me the same question, and I told him I was just an 11-year-old kid and it was impossible to run a mile nonstop. He told me to do it again. I couldn't believe it. Then right before I took off running, he gave me this tip, "Look son, don't stop no matter how much pain you're feeling. You can slow down as much as you want, but just don't stop." I took his advice, and ran the mile nonstop — that day, and every day after that. That translates into fighting and business. If we trained through the excruciating pain, we could fight through it during a championship bout.

In the meantime, Rocky had gotten married. He had become a family man and gotten civilized. He then stopped following the fundamental principles that got him the success he'd attained. This affected his business, and therefore his income. In turn, this put a strain on his marriage and led to divorce. He became depressed shortly after that, and I didn't hear from him for years. This is to say that there is another valuable lesson in boxing: don't forget the basics. When all else fails, you can always rely on them. The jab is the most important punch in boxing. As plain and simple as it may seem, it sets up all the other power punches. If you ever find yourself fighting the other person's fight, take a step back, and go back to the basics. And the same is true in business.

I had become independent of Rocky earlier that year, when he failed to show up to a big meeting we had. He was unintentionally running behind, and told me to take care of the meeting and that he wasn't going to make it. I begged him to show up, even if it were late. He told me he couldn't, and told me I had it, then hung up. Rocky drove a Bentley at the time, and subconsciously, I thought I needed him and the car, in order to close business. But after that day, I knew for a fact that I didn't need him, nor the car, nor anyone or anything for that matter. This empowered me beyond belief. Later in my career, I learned from the book *The Power of the Subconscious Mind* that 90% of our conscious day is controlled by the subconscious mind. I had habitually become dependent on Rocky and his foreign car, but not anymore. I suddenly realized why my coach had me in front of the mirror for two hours a day, six days a week, for the first three months at the gym, just practicing my jab. So that if and when I got into trouble, subconsciously, my instant reflexes would be to go back to the basic fundamentals and I'd be able to jab my way out.

For the first two years in business, I made the conscious choice to abstain from sex, since it turned you into a different animal. In boxing, we're not allowed to have sex up to 3-6 months before a fight. It simply makes you weak and unfocused. Hence, I didn't lose my virginity until I was 17 and almost a senior in high school. Just like when you feed a fighting dog, he loses the next fight because it lost its hunger. Then I finally started dating a girl that I'd known since I first moved into the Brown Sub projects. Everything was going good for the first year and a half, but when it all slowed down a bit, she decided to relocate to NY and we tried having a long-distance relationship. Long story short, we ended up breaking up, she got married and had a kid, and I was left heartbroken. Sometimes, all the personal development in the world can't help you through certain situations in life. During these times you need the right people in your life as a support system. Some people never recover from a tragedy in their life, simply because of who they had in their inner circle during those times. The law of association can make or break you during hardship. Thankfully, I had great people in my life, and I was able to bounce back.

In business, just like in boxing, it is important that you maintain a clear mind before "getting in the ring". What goes on in your personal life will affect you in your professional life 100% of the time, whether you choose to believe it or not. Despite my past associations, to this day I've never smoked or drank, whatsoever. My discipline from boxing overshadowed the influence of my peers. I'll never forget what my coach once told me. He said "Angel, when you get in the ring, your life is at risk. Never risk your life for 20 minutes of pleasure." Business had become my life, and the stage was my ring. I don't even gamble my money, so why would I gamble my goals and dreams?

One of the people in my life that helped me get through my tough times was Jenn, that lady from Vancouver that I had helped years prior. When we first met, it was strictly business for the first year. As a matter of fact, she had been in a relationship for over 12 years. I also had a girlfriend at the time. But when you have a vision for your future and your significant other can't see it, it's easy to drift apart, and that's exactly what happened to both of us. Throughout the years, things went from me helping her, to her helping me, to us helping each other. I started flying from Miami to Vancouver on a quarterly basis. We went from a mentor and mentee relationship to an accountability partnership. In boxing, it's easier to hit the pavement and run the miles when you have someone next to you, pushing you and making sure you don't give up and stop before the finish line. Business is no different; on the road to success, accountability is a major key. One of my billionaire mentors taught me one of the most important questions you could ever ask yourself is what has the lack of accountability cost you in your life?

After mainly building our businesses in our respective hometowns for over 5 years, Jenn and I decided to relocate to another city. Sometimes, if you're feeling stagnant, a change of scenery may help. The challenges that come with relocating will stretch you beyond belief and put your true skills to the test. When you're trying to get fit, you learn that there's such a thing as muscle memory. Meaning that, if you keep doing the same exercises daily, eventually your muscles will get used to them. So every now and then, you should mix it up and confuse your muscles in order to force growth on them. So if you're considering moving out of your hometown, trust me when I say it's a life hack that will minimize your distractions and change your perspective on life.

Jenn and I did some market research, and decided that Houston, TX was the best move for us. I had been developing business there for a few months prior to us having the conversation about relocating, so I knew it was a great market to move to. Jenn took immediate action, and messaged over 30 people on Craigslist, inquiring about short term leases, since we weren't sure where we would settle down. After a whole week, only one person responded, and he was rude to her, so we definitely weren't moving in there. During that same week, three of her mutual friends randomly messaged her on Facebook, suggesting that she should move to Ohio, which was an even better market for our business. After she explained what had happened throughout the week, I gave her the OK to relocate there, and agreed to meet her there within the next 90 days. I had some loose ends I needed to tie up in Miami before taking that final leap of faith.

There's a saying in boxing: "roll with the punches". This simply means that when you see a punch coming your way, just turn your head/body in the same direction that the punch is headed in order to lessen the impact — instead of resisting by turning your head/body against the punch, which would cause the power of the blow to increase. In business, that same philosophy is "trust the process". When things don't go your way, don't argue with the universe, just trust the process and go with the flow. I'd always affirm and repeat, "Everything happens *for* me, nothing happens *to* me."

When Jenn arrived in Cleveland, OH, she took about a week to get settled in and game plan her takeover. By the end of the week, she met with two of her friends that had suggested her relocation. When they went over the number, and showed her how good business really was, she called me immediately and told me I needed to speed up my move. I told her ok, give me a month. Then she went over the numbers with me that Saturday afternoon. I packed my stuff, and was there by Sunday night!

One of the main reasons most people don't succeed in life is because of indecision. Indecision is the thief of opportunity. The inability to decide on any occasion can cause you to live a life of regret and remorse, whether financially or relationally. Successful people make decisions fast and most importantly stick to them, adjusting accordingly to their goals. When you're in a boxing match, every punch comes in a flash, therefore, you must be able to think quick on your feet, within a millisecond, to either move or punch. There's no time to sit and think about what to do next; you just do it. If you choose to sit and ponder in the middle of a fight, you will get punched in the mouth. Luckily, this is just business. The worst thing someone can do is say no to becoming your customer or business partner.

When I arrived in Cleveland, I realized that I didn't know anyone there, nor did I know where to start. See, when you make a decision, it's not always the right decision. The important thing is that you made one, you could always adjust and make it right later. I was just acting on what I had been taught through all my years of training: commit first, and you'll figure out the rest later. When you accept a fight in boxing, there's a high chance, nine times out of ten, you're not at the weight that is required for the match. Yet you accept it, and then get to working out.

Jenn then gave me the suggestion that I start driving an Uber in order to network. I don't smoke nor drink, so a bar wasn't the place for me to network. And I don't gamble, so the local casino was out of the question, too. I was humble enough to take on the role that I needed to in order to get to where I ultimately wanted to be. With the level of success and income I had previously had, most people would let their ego get in the way of their mission and goals. I had learned a long time ago in boxing, never to get too big to do the little things. Sometimes, boxers win a couple of fights in a row and feel that they no longer need to run and hit the pavement at 4 in the morning. But whatever gets you to the top, you must continue to do in order to stay at the top.

The next day I got to work, and then I realized I didn't know much about the Cleveland market. Unlike Miami and Houston, I didn't know the language. I was clueless when it came to the local companies we were brokering for. So we decided to find the best training center in town and go back to being a student. See, growth is never attained, it's always pursued. My boxing coach would always remind me during training sessions that the harder I trained, the easier the fight would be. So after a month and a half of consistently going to basic and leadership trainings, we finally got some traction in this new city. Not only were we back to the top, but our teams got inspired by our bold move and started to follow suit and started producing big results independently of us!

EXPECT THE UNEXPECTED

If You Stay Ready, You Never Have to Get Ready

Many times, during my amateur boxing career, I would train for months, and on fight night my opponent wouldn't show up, causing them to be disqualified, and I would automatically be declared the winner. It's for that same reason that it's important to always show up in business. I see so many people put in the work but never show up when it was time to cash the check. But there were also times when I wasn't scheduled to fight on a particular night, but then a challenger appeared, and I had to gear up to box. Just like in business, where not every meeting/presentation will be the perfect set up. And not every customer will be the ideal referral, but if you stay ready for war, you'll never have to get ready to fight.

I always carried my iPad everywhere I went and made sure my pitch was on point. Because of that mindset, I was able to acquire over one thousand new customers just through driving Uber. My mentor taught me that proper preparation prevents poor performance. And that goes for both boxing and business.

Business is a contact sport, meaning that the more contacts you meet, the more contracts you'll eventually get. Knowing it's all a numbers game, Jenn and I talked to everyone, everywhere we went, in order to tap into the ideal network of business owners. Boxing is also about the numbers. There's a saying that's used by boxers everywhere, "punches in bunches," meaning that the more punches you throw at your opponent, the higher the chances of connecting and scoring points. This world is governed by universal laws, and the law of large numbers will never fail you.

Now, understand this, people follow people with posture and vision, not people with money. With that being said, we weren't going around talking to people without the proper posture. People can smell an out of towner from a mile away, so it was important for us to speak with confidence and dress the part. I learned this the hard way in boxing. If you don't have the proper posture when you're punching, you can and *will* hurt yourself. Not having the proper posture when you're getting hit can cause you to stumble, fall, and even get knocked out. Posture stems from confidence, and confidence comes from knowledge. The only way to get proper knowledge is from training over and over again. For repetition is the mother of learning and the father of all skills.

I recall one of the most valuable experiences I had in the gym, pertaining to posture. I used to always walk around the gym with a slouched back, due to being tired from all the training back to back. Until one day, this guy named BIg Mario, one of the heavyweights in the gym, noticed my posture. He slowly walked up to me and proceeded to punch me with immense power in my chest, knocking the wind out of me, as he yelled "pick your head up and walk straight youngin'". As I gasped for air, I couldn't help but laugh at the way Mario intended to teach me this lesson on posture. He continued to do this, week after week, catching me off guard every time. Thankfully, one day I got the message and decided to walk around the gym with my chest poked out and the proper posture. 'Til this day I am reminded of those blows Big Mario would hit me with, so I continue to walk with my back straightened. Wouldn't it be nice if we all had a Big Mario in our entrepreneurial life, to remind us of when we're not speaking, dealing, and closing business with the proper posture?

Jenn and I experienced a lot of ups and downs during the first few years of relocating. But in business that's to be expected. Not expecting the highs and lows as an entrepreneur is like signing up for boxing lessons and not expecting to get hit. It's inevitable. It's all a mindset, but most people don't have their mind right. If your mindset is right, then nothing else matters. If your mindset is wrong, then nothing else matters. Wherever your mind goes, your body will follow. That's why in boxing there's such a thing as headhunters. These styles of boxers only aim to knock your head off, because they know if they accomplish that, your body will drop with it.

But no matter how many training sessions we attended, or how many challenges we overcame, we couldn't have prepared for the global pandemic of 2020. We had big goals for that year, but in the words of the legendary Mike Tyson, "Everybody has a plan 'til they get punched in the mouth!" That's exactly how we felt. We went from having in-person meetings to having to do everything virtually or over the phone. When the mandatory lockdowns took place, and we were instructed to self-isolate, we had to cancel three events — in three cities and two countries. One event was with the founder of our company, something we had been working on for years to accomplish. It cost us the deposits, as well as our credibility. Our teams were looking to us to see how we were going to pivot and adjust to the circumstances at hand. However, there's a street saying that goes like this, "Never let them see you sweat!"

This is where my boxing attitude helped us through a tough time, once again. Never show doubt, fear, or worry to the people that are following you or competing against you. So many fighters lose a fight before they even get in the ring, from simple intimidation. This was one of Mike Tyson's greatest tactics. He would strategically instil fear in his opponents by staring them down from the moment they stepped in the ring. He would break them mentally first, and then break them physically. So we assured our teams that we had everything under control, and we went at it harder than ever before. We started to focus on the positives and not the negatives. For example, we focused on the fact that we didn't have to pay for flights or hotels. Or that we didn't have to wake up two hours prior to an event to dress up and commute — we could now just plug in from the comfort of our own homes. We did everything we could to lift our team's spirits, yet our income was still cut in half. But we maintained a poker face.

Our business was our sole source of income for over 8 years, and though we did well for ourselves, we knew we had to diversify. Luckily, all the obstacles we had overcome throughout the past decade had turned us into professional problem solvers. Thankfully, we've had great mentors in our lives to guide us during the good, the bad, and the ugly. The right mentors can turn decades of trial and error into days, saving you years of headaches and heartaches. Smart people learn from their own mistakes, wise people learn from the mistakes of others, and dumb people never learn from their mistakes at all.

One of our billionaire mentors suggested we attack the pandemic head on, by investing all of our savings, instead of trying to live off it. Within six months we started six businesses, five which were all in profit. We were now back to making the type of money we were used to, allowing us to focus and adjust to the recent situation and also get our main business back to where we want it to be. All because we were coachable by our mentor and decided to invest in ourselves. See, there's no instrument designed to measure the heart and hunger of a person. The only way you can tell their hunger, is by the urgency with which they apply what their coach has instructed them to do.

As I continue on my journey as an entrepreneur, I can't help but think about all the comeback stories of fighters who were losing, but came back to win in the twelfth round through a knockout. You see this in all sports — in basketball with the game-winning shot, in football with the fourth quarter touchdown... The most important lesson that I learned in boxing that I apply to business every day, is just to never give up! No matter how bad it looks, how down the judges have you on the score cards, or how bad you're hurting, never throw in the towel and quit. Because you never know when things will turn around for you, and you'll have the comeback story of the decade, inspiring millions across the globe as you are crowned world champion in your field, arena, or ring!

When you're in the ring, focus on the task at hand, and that is to hit and not get hit, and ultimately win the fight. In order to concentrate on your opponent, it is imperative that you drown out the noise from the crowd that is either cheering you on or booing you down. Remember to stay on your toes, and be ready to pivot whenever life comes rushing at you out of nowhere. Never take training for granted, because practice doesn't make perfect; it makes improvements. The moment you lose a fight or miss out on a deal, you're going to wish you had trained harder and worked more on your skills. As my favorite boxing quote of all time goes, "It's not the size of the dog in the fight, but the size of the fight in the dog that counts!"

THE VERDICT: AND THE WINNER IS...

Most People See the Glory, but They don't Know the Story

Some people may ask, well, how successful am I, really? My response is that the definition of success is different for every single human being on this planet. Some say success is purely measured by money, and material things. Others say, true success is time and financial freedom, being able to do what you want, when you want, with whomever you want. Some say it should strictly be educational, and success should be solely based on how many degrees one has acquired. A few even say, man's success should never be determined by the amount of objects he's managed to attain, but by the amount of obstacles that man has overcome. I personally believe that success is a little bit of all three of those, plus a little more. Giving back is also an important pillar of success. Whether it's time, money, or knowledge, one should always go back and help those who need it. Once you do that, you'll go from success to significance, the ultimate pinnacle of success.

Given my circumstances, statistically, I'm not supposed to be where I'm at today, or where I'll be tomorrow. Over the last decade, I've consistently worked on my personal growth and development, which has turned my world upside down. I no longer have to carry a gun and look over my shoulder on a daily basis. My circle of friends has evolved to the point where everyone I know is goal oriented, growth focused, big dreamers, and global impact players. I went from having managers, to having over a hundred direct and indirect mentors, worth tens of millions, hundreds of millions, and some even billions of dollars. These mentors stretch me outside of my comfort zone and hold me accountable to my greatness!

Since I've trained my mind to seek out good investments, not just good jobs, I now own 7 businesses and I'm working on developing additional streams of income. I earn more every month than I used to earn all year about ten years ago. And it's all due to the fact that I learned not to work for money, but rather have my money work for me. I've learned to invest in the stock market, real estate, and several other assets that yield passive and residual income, which cover my lifestyle expenses. I now travel back and forth between my two condos in Canada and the US. Jenn and I got married a few years back, and now have a beautiful baby girl, Angelina. We've also been documented multiple times in *Success Magazine* for our achievements over the past years. Combined, we've generated well over ten million dollars in sales so far.

Over the past decade I've spoken in schools, churches, conventions, business meetings, and webinars to over a million people about my story. But most importantly, I'm blessed to say that I've mastered the number one fear known to mankind, public speaking! I have become a master communicator, as well as mastered the highest paying skill, next to being a pro athlete or entertainer: sales. Through consistent training and implementation, I have learned skills so valuable that I will never have to go back to my old ways in order to make money — period.

For years, I was bitter that my boxing career never reached the heights that I wanted it to. I even refused to watch boxing on TV for almost ten years. I couldn't stomach the fact that the same guys that I came up with, or competed against, had now achieved their dreams of becoming world champions, if not top contenders. I would say to myself, I will not watch a boxing match unless I could afford to sit ringside during a championship fight. Today, I no longer think that way. Though I could afford those ringside seats, I understand that I am exactly where I'm supposed to be, doing what God put me here to do. I no longer question what happened to me. Getting shot and being practically homeless and struggling financially, were all the things that were supposed to happen to me. That mess is now my message that I use to inspire tens of thousands of people around the world. Those things were meant to happen so that my story can impact people who have gone or will go through similar situations. Knowing that I was able to grow through what I went through should give those same people the hope they need to keep fighting.

Despite my dark and violent past, I am at peace with who I've become today. I can genuinely say that I have given back to the community more than I have taken from it. I can assure you that all the good that I've done to people definitely outweighs the bad. I help and inspire more people presently than those I terrorized and hurt in the past. I used to change people's lives in a negative way, now I change people's lives in a positive way, and I will continue to do this for the rest of my life. If you were to meet me today and have a conversation with me, you wouldn't be able to tell I've had such a crazy past, unless you've read this book of course. Coaching and mentoring people to overcome challenges, think big, and not let their past control their destiny, has become a true life passion of mine. Entrepreneurship saved my life, and I know for a fact it can do the same for you or anyone who commits to the journey

My boxing coach, Robert Daniels, has since been inducted into the Florida Boxing Hall of Fame. His son, Robert Daniels Jr., is now a pro boxer with hopes of following in his father's footsteps.

Kelvin Witherspoon aka Kel, is now an actor, writer, and movie producer. Don't be surprised if you catch him on the big screen in a theater near you. We are also business partners on several different ventures and still talk every day about who will get to billionaire status first.

Keith Wallace, as we all predicted, went on to become an internet sensation and is now traveling the world performing and making a living off of his music. You might have seen him on social media with one of his viral videos rapping in his car.

Rocky and I have since reconnected, in hopes of doing business together again soon. He has now created his own brand under Rock Did It and is helping others maximize their potential in life and in business.

My mom has been happily remarried for some time now, to a marine vet. She has three grandchildren and still lives in Miami.

As far as my dad is concerned, I got in contact with him about a year ago. I found out that he, his wife, and their three kids were living in extreme poverty in one of the most dangerous slums of Santo Domingo. All five of them were staying in a room in the back of a house, where they had no windows, and no ventilation. They had two beds, full of bugs. A broken TV. A beat-up stove top. A broken fan. And no running water. Only a water well, where they had to scoop water twice a week when it came. Not to mention, a bathroom with no lights, in which they had to share with five other families. He told me no one would hire him in a third world country due to his age. Thankfully, my mentors taught me to always honor my parents no matter what. So I was blessed to be in a position to fly over to the D. R., move him out of where they were living, put him in a two story, 5 bed 2 bath house, and furnish it with all new appliances. Since he couldn't find a job, I helped him open up a business out of his house, where he can cook and sell food. Now he no longer has to try to survive, but he can live and thrive with his family. He's now able to support them, as well as fend for himself with the income from the business. I also bought him a minibus, so he wouldn't have to walk 4 miles round trip to the market at his age. You can see the pictures of everything on my Instagram @iamangelcarmona.

Oh, and House Of Wings is still the best chicken spot in Miami! They relocated to downtown Miami and are still serving the best wings in town.

FINAL THOUGHT

Many people see the glory, but don't know the story, until now. For years, I would start my speeches by saying "I'm just a regular guy, with extraordinary dreams", but I was far from a regular guy. As the saying goes, every saint has a past and every sinner has a future. I wrote this book to show that success is the same in all areas of life. No matter the sport, the principles to become a champion can be applied across the board. Business is the ultimate sport, and money and impact is how we keep score. I truly hope this book helps thousands, if not millions of athletes around the world, in any sport, become successful entrepreneurs. I also wish this book encourages you to tell your story of how you went from being a good athlete to a great business person, so that you may inspire those in alignment with your chain of destiny.

As I travel telling my story, I always get asked, if I loved boxing so much, why didn't I go back after I fully healed?. The truth of the matter is, that I am genuinely happy where

I'm at in my life. I wholeheartedly feel as if business is my new arena. My coach would always tell me, boxing is 80% mental and 20% physical, but it took me becoming an entrepreneur to fully understand what he meant all along. I still workout 3-5 times a week just to maintain my physique. If for whatever reason I ever decide to box again, I know for a fact I would be twice as good as before because of the mindset that I've developed as a businessman.

I challenge you to make your goals and dreams a sport. When you do this you will force yourself to find a coach to help you succeed. And if you have any level of competitiveness in you, I assure you the chances of you winning at this sport will increase dramatically. The only advantage I would say I had over most people who fail in business or never did any sports, is my ability to be coachable to people who are where I want to be and have an outside perspective. My second advantage is being disciplined beyond measures. I advise you to make sure your environment is conducive to your goals and dreams. Always keep in mind that you won't get much accomplished if you only grind on the days that you feel good. With that being said, I'll leave you with one of my favorite quotes from one of my mentors…

"In life you are guaranteed to suffer one of two pains, the pain of discipline or the pain of regret. The pain of discipline will last but a moment, yet the pain of regret is eternal!"
– Jim Rohn

Angel Carmona
CEO · SPEAKER · AUTHOR

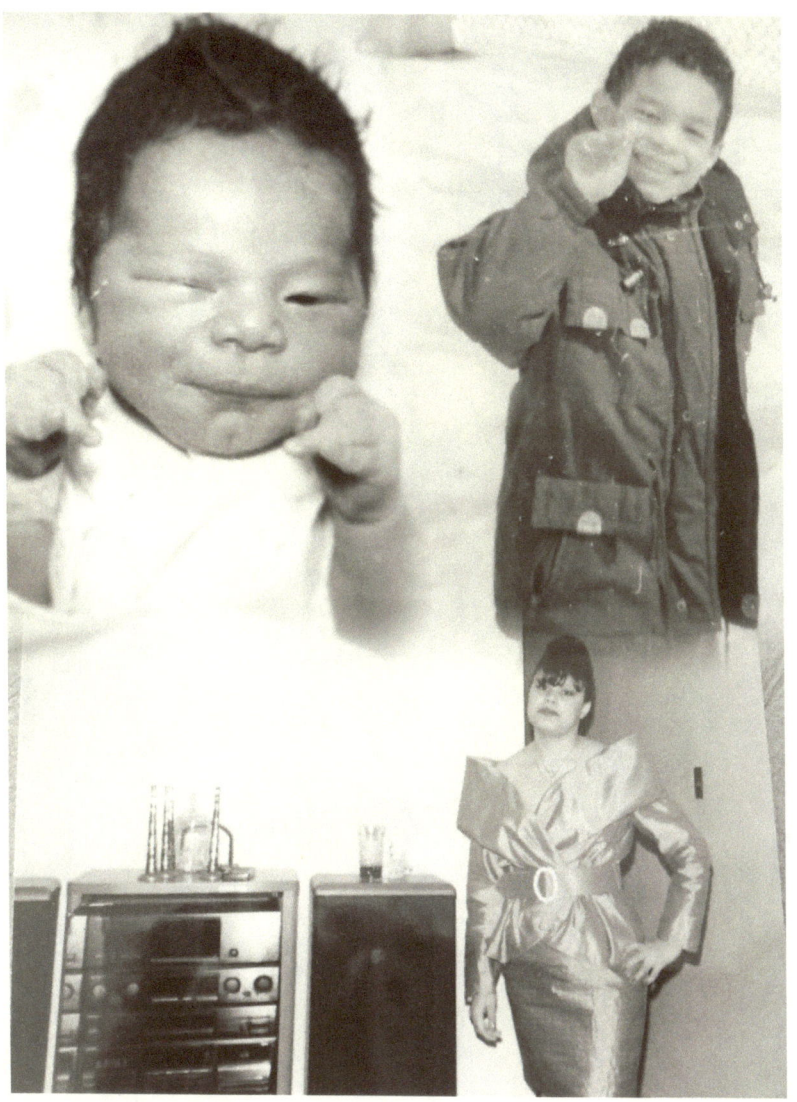

A champion was born. Life in NY. My mom.

My Family in Santo Domingo, DR

My dad & my God mother

Rocky & Me our first day at the gym VS years later as champions

Me in the hood.

Our Mixtape cover. Keith, Kel, & Myself.
A pic after we hit a lick. One of my mugshots.

My transition into business

Jenn & Me

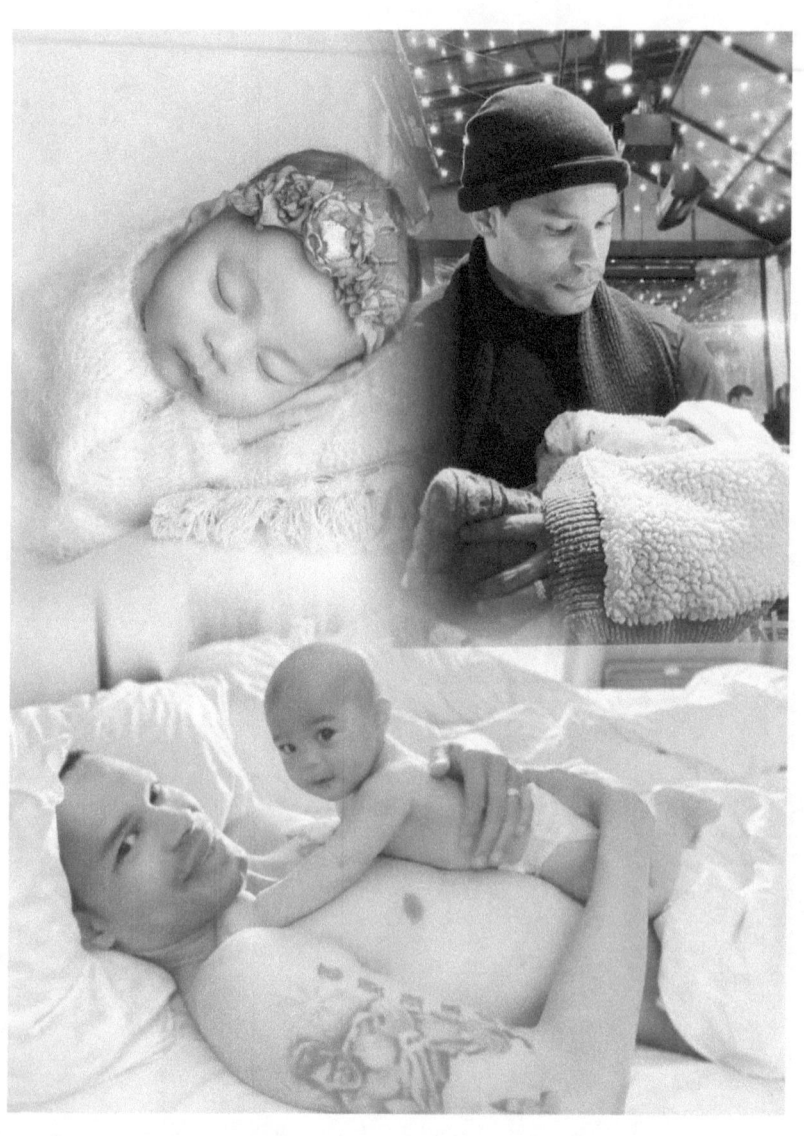

My dad & me in 2020 with the business I helped him start.

www.ingramcontent.com/pod-product-compliance
Lightning Source LLC
LaVergne TN
LVHW041957060526
838200LV00018B/373/J